The Russian Empire

A Captivating Guide to the Third-Largest Empire in History, Starting from Peter the Great to the Russian Revolution

Free Bonus from Captivating History
(Available for a Limited time)

Hi History Lovers!

Now you have a chance to join our exclusive history list so you can get your first history ebook for free as well as discounts and a potential to get more history books for free! Simply visit the link below to join.

Captivatinghistory.com/ebook

Also, make sure to follow us on Facebook, Twitter and Youtube by searching for Captivating History.

Contents

Introduction: The First Manifestations of Russian Power

The Russian Empire spanned a vast territory, which, at its height, stretched from Poland all the way to the Pacific. This empire encompassed millions of people and cultures all throughout the entire Eurasian continent. The official start date of this empire is debatable. While some cite its origins as being as far back as 1450, others insist that the Russian Empire did not truly begin until 1721 under the auspices of that often-praised champion of Russian history, Peter the Great.

But regardless of the exact start date, in order to understand how Russian imperial might came to be, one must go back even further, to the very founding of Russia itself. Russia originates from the Rus' people, who settled a region that roughly corresponds to modern-day Russia in 862 CE. Roughly one hundred years later, the region strengthened its ties with the Byzantine Empire—the Christian bulwark of Eastern Europe—and made Christianity its official religion in 988 CE.

This manifestation of early Russian power was largely disrupted in the 13th century due to the rise of the Mongol horde in the East. First, Genghis Khan and then his successors rampaged through much of Asia, the Middle East, and Eastern Europe. The early Russian state did not effectively recover until the late 1400s. This was the time when Russia really came into its own. And from here on out, the Russian state would rise from the ashes of the Mongol khanate to become the greatest juggernaut of the Eurasian sphere.

It is really no coincidence that it was just as Russia's Orthodox Christian mentors—the Byzantine Empire—collapsed that the Russian Empire began to rise up. The Byzantine Empire was the successor kingdom of the Roman Empire; the Byzantines' capital of Constantinople (modern-day Istanbul) was known as the second Rome. The Byzantine Empire was defeated by the Ottoman Turks in 1453. With this defeat, the second Rome of Christendom was lost, and Constantinople ultimately became Istanbul, Turkey.

The Russians, in the meantime, looked upon their own great city of Moscow as the "Third Rome." And the fact that Russia was now the major Orthodox Christian power made the Russians feel that they were the direct inheritors of the Roman Empire. Russian leaders even titled themselves as "tsar," which was the Roman equivalent of "Caesar."

It was during the reign of Russian Tsar Ivan III that the idea of Moscow being the third Rome would really crystalize. And the sentiment was most famously captured in an epistle written to him by one of his most faithful monks—Filofei of Pskov. Filofei wrote, "This present church of the third, new Rome, of thy sovereign Empire: The Holy Catholic Apostolic Church...shines in the whole universe more resplendent than the sun. And let it be known to the Lordship, oh pious Tsar, that all the empires of the Orthodox Christian faith have converged into thine one Empire. Thou art the sole Emperor of all the Christians in the whole universe. For two Romes have fallen, the third stands, and there shall be no fourth."

Yes, according to Filofei, Rome and Constantinople, two cities that claimed to be the center of Roman imperial might, had fallen. Yet Moscow still stood, and Filofei predicted it would remain standing since there would not be a "fourth" to rise up after it. Ivan III was the first Russian monarch to take up this mantle, calling himself a "tsar" and even marrying a Byzantine princess—Sophia Palaiologina—who was the niece of the last Byzantine emperor, Constantine XI.

This marriage, which officially entered the Russian royalty into the bloodlines of Byzantium itself, was believed to have sealed Russia's fate as the successor of the Byzantine Empire. After Ivan III's marriage to Sophia, Russia even began to use the "double-headed eagle," which had long been a symbol of Byzantium.

Ivan III's marriage to Sophia also proved beneficial in forging a more powerful military. Sophia, you see, had been raised in Rome on the hospitality of the pope. As such, she had developed long-lasting ties with Italy. These connections enabled Ivan III to reach out to Italian arms makers in 1494, who then came to Russia and established a cannon and powder-making factory. Ivan also had Italian engineers help him improve Russian fortifications so that they would be able to stand up against the cannons of enemy forces. This was important to the Russians since it was largely the cannons of the Ottoman Turks that spelled the end for the Byzantines in 1453.

Ivan III's marriage to Sophia was indeed a convenient one, but besides all of these pragmatic benefits, it seems that Ivan truly did love his wife, so much so, in fact, that the considerable care he took to make sure she remained safe while he was away on military campaigns occasionally led to criticism among his military commanders.

At any rate, in this new arrangement of Russian proto-imperial might, Ivan III would reign quite successfully until the year 1505. After Ivan III's rule came to an end, his son, Vasili III, took his place at the helm. Vasili built upon the foundation laid by his father, allowing the bulk and power of the Russian army to be enhanced considerably. This army was used to expand Russian imperial might in all directions. These new swaths of territories then proved their worth in gold, as they allowed the establishment of municipalities to which the best and brightest would be drawn.

The holding of these lands, of course, did not come easy, and it required the establishment of even more defensive fortifications, which meant the expenditure of more money and manpower to maintain them. During Vasili III's reign, the biggest thorn in his side proved to be Crimea. Russia did not control this piece of territory in those days, and in 1521, the warlords of Crimea teamed up with the khanate inheritors of Genghis Khan in the region of Astrakhan.

These supposed heirs of the so-called "Golden Horde" banded together to launch a blistering offensive. They relentlessly drove their forces from the south and the east, and they almost managed to march on Moscow in the process. In fact, the enemy troops came so close to overrunning Moscow that Vasili III had to be temporarily evacuated. The Russians would rally, however, and push back the aggressors.

In the meantime, Vasili III had another crisis to contend with on the domestic front: he was in desperate need of an heir. Every king, emperor, and potentate of all stripes needed to have an heir to ensure the continuation of their dynasty. Vasili had wed a woman named Solomonia Saburova, but by the time of their twentieth wedding anniversary in 1526, she had yet to produce a child.

It is distressing to any couple to find that they have difficulty conceiving, and nowadays, much sensitivity is given to the subject. In Ivan's day, however, it was seen as a valid excuse to get rid of an old wife in favor of a new one. Ivan did this, marrying a much younger woman by the name of Elena Glinskaya. After a few years of trying, Elena finally produced an heir for Vasili in the form of Ivan IV or, as this powerful Russian monarch would one day be better known, Ivan the Terrible.

Chapter 1 – Ivan the Terrible and the Foundations of the Empire

"A man who lies to himself, and believes his own lies, becomes unable to recognize truth, either in himself or in anyone else, and he ends up losing respect for himself and for others. When he has no respect for anyone, he can no longer love, and, in order to divert himself, having no love in him, he yields to his impulses, indulges in the lowest form of pleasure, and behaves in the end like an animal in satisfying his vices. And it all comes from lying—to others and to yourself."

-Fyodor Dostoevsky

Ivan IV, or as he is otherwise known, Ivan the Terrible, was born around the year 1530. His father Vasili III would perish just a few years later, succumbing to a painful and apparently fatal abscess in his hip. The unstoppable infection of this abscess took Vasili's life on December 3rd, 1533. This left three-year-old Ivan IV as the would-be-emperor, but obviously, a three-year-old would not be able to govern an empire.

As such, it fell upon Empress Elena Glinskaya, along with court advisors, to shield and steward the young monarch until he came of age. Glinskaya proved to be an able stateswoman in her own right, and it is said that she helped to unify the currency of the empire by means of promoting internal trade and streamlining the process of taxation. But her influence was destined to be short-lived.

Sadly enough, in 1538, when Ivan was only seven years old, Elena would abruptly perish. She was around twenty-eight years old at the time, and due to the mysterious nature of her demise, many have openly wondered if perhaps she had been murdered. At any rate, Ivan was now at the mercy of court officials.

In many ways, it is perhaps a bit extraordinary that Ivan was even allowed to grow up and become emperor. In many other instances in history, when a presumptive heir is bereft of their parents and still too young to take the throne, the youth was pushed aside in favor of a usurper. Yet, in Ivan's case, no court intriguer managed to deny Ivan his right to one day ascend to the throne. However, according to Ivan's later testimony, his stewards did not treat him very well.

Ivan would later claim that as a child, his supposed guardians would lock him up in a room for most of the day, only letting him out to attend special ceremonies at court. He felt more like a prisoner than a prince, and Ivan would recall how he slammed his fist into the heavy wooden door of his bedroom, begging to be let out, only for his cries to be left unheard. This isolation would not come to an end until January 16th, 1547, for it was that year that sixteen-year-old Ivan was finally handed the crown that would make him tsar.

Although Ivan had been isolated for much of his youth, he was suddenly thrust into the role of head of state, and events moved rather rapidly for the young tsar. Shortly after he was crowned, he married Anastasia Romanovna on February 3rd, 1547. It was from this union that the Romanov dynasty would spring, a lineage that would continue until the deaths of the last Russian royal family in the early 20th century.

The fact that Ivan married so early is probably an indication of dynastic concern, as well as a young man long deprived of intimacy. It is quite likely that he desperately needed a close companion with whom to share his life. This orphan king had no one else to turn to, so he would make his wife Anastasia be his closest, ready-made confidant. And he would need her support just a few months into their marriage when he had to deal with the first major crisis of his reign. That June, Moscow literally erupted in flames when an out-of-control blaze managed to destroy much of the capital's downtown.

It is thought that thousands died and that tens of thousands were made homeless due to the inferno. Although the fire seems to have been an accident, the people almost immediately turned their wrath on the young tsar. Bizarrely enough, some even blamed Ivan IV's long-deceased mother, Elena Glinskaya. According to the local gossips, she was a witch and had placed a curse on the city before she died. While her mysterious death has indeed made many wonder if a court minister might have slipped her some poison, the idea of her engaging in sorcery with her dying breath sounds pretty absurd.

But the people were angry and ready to believe just about anything as they dug their homes and belongings out of the rubble. As the populace erupted in mass rioting, Ivan was ushered to a suburb of Moscow by his court ministers. He was placed in a remote estate in an attempt to keep him safe from the crowds. However, it was not long before the rabble-rousers figured out where Ivan had fled. Soon, they were marching onto the estate in force, demanding to have an audience with the tsar.

Ivan tried to address the crowd, but his inexperience and apparent timidity only emboldened the rioters further. Pretty soon, they seemed to be on the verge of rushing the tsar so that they could do with him as they pleased. It was not his royal bodyguard or the Russian army who saved him from the clutches of the angry citizenry but rather an old, wizened holy man by the name of Sylvester. The old preacher suddenly stood between Ivan IV and the crowd, and he reminded them that Christianity's most important virtue is forgiveness. Sylvester told them that even if the tsar was somehow at fault, it was incumbent upon them as Christians to enable the monarch to repent.

After Sylvester's words, Ivan actually knelt before the riotous crowd and asked them to forgive him for his perceived shortcomings.

Amazingly enough, the sight of the young tsar laying prostrate before them managed to quell the fires of their rage. And soon, rather than wanting to exact vengeance upon their emperor, those in the crowd actually felt sorry for Ivan. As such, the previously angry group began to turn around and left in peace, willing to forgive and forget. With this crisis averted, Ivan worked to better consolidate his hold on power. He centralized much of the bureaucracy, and he made improvements to the Russian military.

This military buildup would continue over the next several years, laying the groundwork for a major military offensive in 1552. That year, the tsar sent around 150,000 of his soldiers toward Kazan to take on one of the last remnants of the Golden Horde that the Mongols had left behind. Kazan was a heavily fortified city in southwestern Russia. It was placed upon a hill and had a moat surrounding it. Russia had been building up its cannons and other heavy artillery for decades, and it would need all the firepower it could get to break down the walls of Kazan.

The Kazan people, though inheritors of Mongol might, were actually of Turkic extraction and practiced the Islamic faith. The Russians had long referred to them as "Tartars" and had been plotting to subdue them for quite some time. Initially, the assault on Kazan proved to be slow going, as the walls held up fairly well against Russian arms. Making matters worse, a terrible rainstorm erupted during the assault, which made the ground muddy and almost impossible to traverse, with Russian soldiers slipping and sliding all over the terrain.

According to Russian legend, the troops took the storm clouds as a bad omen. In order to circumvent it, Russian commanders are said to have hauled out the holy relic of the "True Cross." Ever since the days of Constantine the Great—the first Christian Roman emperor—there have been legends that fragments of the True Cross, on which Christ was crucified, had been recovered. Allegedly, some of these splintered pieces of wood had been incorporated with a traditional Russian cross, and it was this cross that the Russian army held aloft on that stormy day.

According to legend, as soon as this relic of the True Cross was raised high over their heads, the storm suddenly subsided. The clouds parted, and radiant rays of sunlight came streaming forth. This was apparently enough to reinvigorate the Russian soldiers, who charged the fortress of Kazan. The Tartars of Kazan were ultimately defeated on October 2nd, 1552.

This was not just blanket conquest by the Russians; it was, in many ways, also a defensive maneuver. After all, the Tartar raids launched from Kazan had kept previous Russian monarchs awake at night, wondering when and where Tartar raiding parties might strike next. As such, it was of great strategic importance for the Russians to gain control of this region in order to bring greater stability to their domain. Many Russians had been kidnapped by Tartar raids and brought back as slaves to Kazan. In fact, the Slavic peoples of Russia had suffered so much from these slavers that the word "slave" itself is thought to have been derived from the "Slavic" people or "Slavs" of Russia. For them, Ivan was the one who had set them free, and his victory over Kazan brought a certain dignity to Russian might.

Just a couple of years later, Ivan IV would launch yet another offensive against the Tartars, this time even farther south, against the Tartar stronghold of Astrakhan. Astrakhan rested on the passage that led to the Caspian Sea. Seizing this port was undoubtedly important for Russia since it would finally grant the Russians access to the sea and allow for the establishment of a proper navy.

On August 29th, 1554, tens of thousands of Russian soldiers poured into the region to take on the Tartars of Astrakhan. The offensive was a smashing success, leaving Russia in complete control over both the Volga River and the Caspian Sea. With these important gains in the east, Ivan would then look to expand his empire to the west. These efforts would lead to the Livonian War.

In order to understand the Livonian War, one must first understand Livonia itself. You see, the long-defunct state of Livonia was an amalgamation of territories in Eastern Europe that had been seized by the so-called "Livonian Knights." The Livonian Knights, or as they were otherwise known, the Livonian Brothers of the Sword, was a military order of knights that had been established by Pope Innocent III in 1204. Just like the Knights Templar, the Hospitallers, and the Teutonic Knights, the Livonian Knights were a crusading order sanctioned by the Catholic Church.

But the mission of the Livonian Knights was much different from the Templars and the Hospitallers. Instead of being sent to the Middle East to do battle against Muslim armies, these crusaders were dispatched to Eastern Europe to root out paganism. Yes, although Russia had become Christian, there were many pagan holdouts in Eastern Europe among the Baltic states. The Teutonic Knights had also been given a similar mission—brutally stamping out paganism in Eastern Europe. In 1236, the Livonian Knights essentially combined with the Teutonic Knights, but they were still considered a distinct organization of their own and referred to as the Livonian Order.

At any rate, the state of Livonia was founded by these knights after they conquered the pagan territories of what today constitutes Latvia and Estonia. It was this territory administered by these crusading knights that Ivan IV wished to seize for himself. Ivan sent his army to take on Livonia in 1558. At first, Ivan was quite successful in putting the Livonian Knights on the defensive, but the Russian march was halted in 1560 at the city of Revel, where a resurgent Livonian force managed to push the Russians back. And after Denmark, Sweden, and Poland were all brought into the war, the waters were muddied enough that this quagmire would ultimately drag on all the way until 1583.

The year 1560 may have been the major turning point in what would amount to a twenty-five-year struggle. That same year would also prove to be a major turning point in Ivan's own personal life, as his soulmate, Anastasia, died. She passed in a similarly sudden and mysterious manner as his mother had. And just like his deceased mother, who perished around the age of twenty-eight, Anastasia Romanovna also died fairly young, at the age of thirty.

It has been said that the brutal Livonian War and the loss of his precious wife changed Ivan's temperament. From here on out, his character became grim and gruff. Ivan's expressions were so dour and his wrath so great that he was commonly referred to as "Grozny," which roughly translated in English means "Terrible."

Ivan managed to overcome his grief somewhat by the following year, for he remarried. His second wife, Maria Temryukovna, was a princess from the southern Caucasus region. She would not last very long as Ivan's wife either; she abruptly perished in 1569—a death that is once again shrouded in mystery and believed to have been the result of poisoning.

The year 1571 proved to be an even darker one for Ivan, as bloody revolts broke out in recently conquered Kazan and Astrakhan. This forced the Russians to fight wars on two fronts; they struggled against the Livonians in the northwest and the Tartar Muslims in the southeast. The pressure would continue to build over the years, and when the Russian military was handed a heavy defeat on the Livonian front in 1578, Ivan was forced to come to the table to negotiate with his enemies.

However, the talks fell through, and in 1579, Russia was once again fighting on the western front. This time, the combined might of Polish, German, and Transylvanian troops managed to overrun the Russians, and they seized the Russian settlement of Polotsk. Ivan was desperate at this point, so desperate, in fact, that he sent an envoy to Rome to speak with the pope.

Ivan's envoy let the pope know that he was ready to do the unthinkable, at least in most Russians' eyes. If the pope would simply call off the crusaders, Ivan promised the pope that he would have his entire realm convert to Catholicism.

Ever since the fall of Constantinople, Russia had presented itself as the guardian of what remained of the Orthodox Church. Now, Ivan was willing to throw all of that away simply to get the pope to sign off on a peace agreement. The Russian public would obviously not be very happy with the result.

But as it turns out, they did not have much to worry about. Ivan was merely using all of this as a ruse to buy more time. Ivan sent an envoy to the Vatican in 1581, and the topic of conversion to Catholicism was mentioned, but even more tantalizing for the pope was the mention of a united Christian front against the Ottoman Empire.

The pope was intrigued, and he immediately offered his services to negotiate peace between the Catholic crusaders and the Russian Empire, with the war ultimately coming to a close in 1583. Ivan lost much of his gains, but he at least managed to save a little face. And it was just in time, as Ivan himself would perish the following year, 1584. The fact that Ivan IV managed to tie up the loose ends of the Livonian War, no matter how disastrous the campaign was for Russia, would enable his successor to step onto the stage with a fresh hand to play.

Chapter 2 – A Time of Troubles and the Founding of Dynasty

"I have outlasted all desire. My dreams and I have grown apart. My grief alone is left entire. The gleamings of an empty heart. The storms of ruthless dispensation have struck my flowery garland numb. I live in lonely desolation and wonder when my end will come. Thus on a naked tree-limb, blasted by tardy winter's whistling chill, a single leaf which has outlasted its season will be trembling still."

-Alexander Pushkin

After his death in 1584, Ivan IV was succeeded by his son, Feodor I. Feodor was actually Ivan's second-oldest son. The reason behind his placement is one of the darkest in Russian history. Feodor became the next in line to the throne because Ivan had killed his own eldest son years earlier with his own hands. Yes, in one of the most shocking scenes in history, Ivan killed his own son, Ivan Ivanovich, in a drunken rage. And by all accounts, as terrible as Ivan's actions were, they were not even in the least bit justified.

The argument had been brought about after Ivan the Terrible had basically attacked his son's wife, Yelena Sheremeteva, for alleged immodesty at court. In other words, Ivan did not like the clothes she was wearing, so he resorted to violence. And when we say attack, we mean attack. He struck her repeatedly, and it is said that his blows even caused her to have a miscarriage.

So, let us consider things from Ivan Ivanovich's perspective. His father has just beat up his wife and very likely caused the death of his own unborn son. Ivan Ivanovich would obviously be distressed about all of this, and like any person, he would want to confront the perpetrator of these heinous acts, which just so happened to be his own father.

Yet, for daring to even question his own dad's ruthless acts, he, in turn, was struck down. Ivan is said to have taken his thick wooden staff and hit Ivan Ivanovich in the head with such force that he was immediately down for the count. For daring to stand up to his own father, Ivan Ivanovich lost his life.

Thus, when Ivan IV himself died in 1584, he was succeeded by Feodor I. Feodor was young and inexperienced, and he would essentially be only a puppet ruler, while Boris Godunov, the chief of the secret police and Feodor's own brother-in-law, called the shots from behind the scenes. Russia began to decline at this point, and the economy began to seriously falter.

Godunov, who acted as regent, tried his best to issue reforms that brought stability to the empire. Feodor, in the meantime, though generally liked by the people, shrunk further and further into the shadows, allowing Boris to rule in his stead. Feodor ultimately died in 1598 without an heir, leaving the question of succession open once again. It was at this moment that Boris decided to seize power for himself. And for the first time, a man outside of the dynastic line was crowned tsar on September 1ˢᵗ, 1598.

This moment would usher in a very difficult period in Russian history known as the "Time of Troubles." In 1598, the Russian economy was still struggling, and many peasants were literally fleeing from their landlords. In order to address this problem, Tsar Godunov tried to lower taxation to lessen the burden on the lower classes. The previous year, he had attempted a much heavier-handed approach to coerce the peasants to remain on the land by issuing a decree that stated they could actually be forced to go back to the landlords on whose land they had toiled.

This was the general pattern of Godunov's rule. It was only when the stick did not work that he would try the carrot. Since he could not force the peasants to stay put, he tried to bribe them to remain in place through tax breaks. During this period, Godunov was also hard at work trying to bring both the Russian military and the Russian bureaucracy up to par with the more modern regimes of Europe. The reforms were slow going, and after suffering through a famine in 1601, Godunov had even more to worry about.

It has been said that crops failed to grow from 1601 to 1602 due to an extremely brutal winter that rocked most of Russia. This caused the starving peasant class to take to the streets, demanding a solution to their problems. The protesters posed a grave threat of insurrection since it seemed that they could turn violent at any moment. In 1604, a group of Russian rebels rose up under the leadership of one Grigorii Otrepev in an attempt to drive the tsar from power.

In the midst of all of this terrible infighting, Godunov abruptly perished, doing so in the spring of 1605. Godunov had no heir, leaving Russia once again in a crisis of succession. It was into this mess that the rebel leader Grigorii Otrepev stepped. Grigorii, you see, had claimed to have been Ivan's long-lost son Dmitrii (also spelled as Dmitry). Dmitrii was dead, yet this man pretended that he was Dmitrii, alive and well. Some believed him, and some did not, but whatever the case was, he became the tsar. However, his reign was exceedingly short, as he was assassinated in May of 1606.

Grigorii was succeeded by a wealthy noble of the boyar class named Vasili Shuisky. Just about as soon as Vasili rose to the throne, a major uprising took place. Vasili was able to put the revolt down by enlisting the aid of Poland, whose troops were enough to turn the tide back in favor of the tsar. However, Vasili's reign was just not meant to last, and after mounting pressure brought on by the sheer discontent of the populace, he was forced to resign in 1610.

It was at this point that the Russian government truly reached a crisis of epic proportions. The boyar class attempted to save their interests by hedging their bets on a Polish prince by the name of Wladyslaw. This only enraged the Russian people, as they had a strong "anti-Polish" bent at the time. It was strong enough, in fact, to lead to the making of the so-called "anti-Polish army" in 1611. This armed mob managed to seize Moscow in 1612, forcing the Assembly of the Land (or as it is called in Russian, the Zemsky Sobor) to elect Mikhail (Michael) Romanov as the new tsar.

Mikhail Romanov, as his last name might give away, was descended from Ivan IV's first wife, Anastasia Romanovna, and he was indeed of royal blood. The crowning of Mikhail Romanov allowed the Russian dynasty to reconstitute itself after several years of turmoil and pretenders to the imperial throne. Mikhail proved to be a popular pick with the common people, as they longed for a return to the stability of a dynastic autocrat. Mikhail was handed the crown in July of 1613, and he immediately went to work on mending the shattered fences of Russian society.

Interestingly enough, his father, Feodor, was also given an important role. He was made the patriarch of the Russian Orthodox Church in 1619, taking on the name "Filaret." This would create a powerful father and son duo, with the son in charge of the state and the father in charge of the church. Some have even gone as far as to suggest that, at least in the beginning, Filaret was the real power behind the throne until his passing in 1633.

At any rate, the Romanov dynasty would continue in force for over three hundred years, from 1613 all the way to 1917. It only came to an end when Russian communists slaughtered the Romanov family during the Russian Revolution. As it pertains to this first member of the reconstituted Romanov line—Mikhail Romanov—his first task was to see to it that all the troops from other nations were made to leave Russian soil.

Various European powers had bankrolled different factions during Russia's civil conflict, but Mikhail was determined to make sure that these outsiders stopped hedging their bets at the expense of Russian blood. Mikhail was able to get Swedish troops to withdraw in the spring of 1617 by agreeing to let go of Russia's toehold in the Baltic region on the Neva River.

Then, in the following year of 1618, an armistice was signed with another foreign antagonist to Russia—Poland. This treaty guaranteed peace with the Polish state for at least another fourteen years. The peace treaty came at a steep cost, however, as it stipulated that the Russians give up yet even more territory; this time, it was the important outpost of Smolensk. Russia seemed to be an empire contracting in on itself, but at least its overall sovereignty had been restored. Mikhail would spend the better part of three decades consolidating Russian power.

During this period, there was also an embrace of so-called "foreign experts," who were welcomed to Russia as a means of speeding up the nation's modernization. One of the most well-known of these foreign experts was the Dutchman Andries Winius, who helped Russia install a major ironworks facility in 1632. For many in the Russian military, who were seeking a build-up of armaments, the timing could not have been better. That very year, the clock ran out on Russia's armistice with Poland.

Not long after, the Russian military attempted to recover the lost city of Smolensk, but their efforts ultimately fell flat. Russia's latest defeat then resulted in yet another peace treaty being forged between the two warring parties, which went into effect in 1634. This treaty sought to punish Russia, and it forced the Russian tsar to agree to not only disavow any claim to Smolensk but also fork over some twenty thousand rubles in reparations.

This latest failure only convinced the Russians to redouble their efforts of modernization since they knew that it was the "backwardness" of their military that was holding them back. Mikhail would continue to pursue such reforms until his death in 1645. Mikhail Romanov was succeeded to the throne by his son, Aleksey (Alexis) Mikhailovich. Aleksey was only sixteen years old when he came to power, but he was an energetic and able leader from a relatively young age.

Initially, however, he placed much of the day-to-day operations in the hands of his advisor and brother-in-law, Boris Morozov. The situation was indeed very much similar to that other infamous Boris—Boris Godunov—who had served as regent on the eve of the Time of Troubles. But when Boris Morozov began to create discontent among the masses through unpopular taxation and heavy-handed policies, which provoked unrest, Aleksey did not hesitate to give his brother-in-law the ax.

He dismissed Boris and then held a special council to actually consider the problems of his subjects and the best methods for correcting them. This resulted in plans to enact fairer taxation, but it also implemented an increase in the landowners' power over the serfs who labored for them. The serfs were essentially enslaved to their landlords, with no means to escape their serfdom.

Even as the serfs were being shackled to the land, Russia's borders were expanding in the north and east through new acquisitions made in Siberia. These inroads would actually lead to a brief conflict with China, as border skirmishes erupted in the Amur Basin over territory claimed by China's Qing dynasty. The pushback that the Russians received resulted in a halt to further expansion toward Chinese territory.

Along with extraterritorial advances, Aleksey also had to deal with domestic turmoil. A major insurrection took place in 1668 when a bunch of monks at a monastery on the Solovetsky Islands decided that they did not like the new prayer books that the Russian state had just commissioned for the church. It may not seem like a big deal to us in the modern world, but back then, even a small change of church routine could spark dire protest.

These monks refused to accept the new prayer books and sent Aleksey a missive that read, in part, "We all wish to die in the old faith, in which your lordship's father, the true-believing lord, Tsar and Grand Prince Mikhail Fedorovich of all Russia and the other true-believing Tsars and Grand Princes lived out their days."

Aleksey was not about to take this insubordination, and he sent his soldiers to the monk's island fortress. The monks refused to grant the troops access to their facility, and incredibly enough, the monks holed themselves up for what would amount to an eight-year siege. This drama only came to an end when the compound was stormed in January of 1676; almost all of those inside were killed. Tsar Aleksey would actually perish himself the following month.

After Aleksey's death, the fifteen-year-old Feodor III (sometimes anglicized as Theodore) came to the throne. Feodor was the eldest son of Aleksey, and he was expected to follow closely in his father's footsteps. Feodor was young, of course, and would require guidance. Making matters even more difficult for the new tsar was the fact that he suffered from a childhood malady that had left him with partial paralysis.

Nevertheless, young Feodor would do his best to rise above his circumstances, and at the outset, he seemed to be doing as well as his predecessors had done. In the summer of 1680, Feodor wed an upper-class Russian lady by the name of Agafya Grushetskaya. He had supposedly met Agafya during a religious procession. During the procession, it is said that some sort of religious reenactment took place in which a character played the part of a witch. The play supposedly startled Agafya, so much so, in fact, that she fainted. It was none other than Feodor who came to the damsel's rescue. The two were said to have fallen in love with each other shortly thereafter. A courtship ensued, and they married.

But this fairytale romance did not end happily ever after. The tsar's wife would give birth to a son in 1681, and she would perish in childbirth. Feodor's and the tsarina's child—the heir to the Russian throne—would perish just one week later.

Feodor's health was failing him, and he knew he needed an heir. So, he married again in 1682, this time to Marfa Apraksina. Feodor would pass away from long-standing health problems just a few months later with no heir apparent. This led to the imperial throne going to the next in line, which was Feodor's younger brother Ivan. However, the succession would soon come into dispute, as some preferred Ivan's half-brother, Peter. In the end, only one would emerge the victor—and he would be called "great."

Chapter 3 – Peter the Great and His Immediate Successors

"Born, the Man assumes the name and image of humanity, and becomes in all things like unto other men who dwell upon the earth. Their hard lot becomes his, and his, in turn, becomes the lot of all who shall come after him. Drawn on inexorably by time, it is not given him to see the next rung on which his faltering foot shall fall. Bounded in knowledge, it is not given him to foretell what each succeeding hour, what each succeeding minute, shall have in store for him. In blind nescience, in an agony of foreboding, in a whirl of hopes and fears, he completes the sorry cycle of an iron destiny."

-Leonid Andreyev

After Tsar Feodor III's passing, the line of succession fell upon his younger brother Ivan. Ivan, however, proved to be a problematic choice since he was only fifteen years old and apparently plagued with even more health problems than Feodor. It was for this reason that the more clear-minded administrators in the Russian Empire began to look at Feodor's half-brother Peter instead. Peter was only ten years old at the time, but he presented a stark contrast to Ivan. Unlike Ivan, Peter was healthy, rambunctious, and full of life.

For court administrators dreading a repeat of the problems they had with Feodor III, Peter seemed like the most logical pick to carry on the dynastic role of imperial monarch. One of the early vocal supporters of Peter was none other than the patriarch of the Russian Orthodox Church. When this religious figure spoke, Russians listened, so when the patriarch spoke about the issue in front of a large crowd in Red Square, the people demanded that Peter be given the crown.

However, Ivan had a strong and determined supporter in the form of his elder sister Sophia, who wished to have her brother installed on the throne in order to be able to curry more favor for herself. It was Sophia's influence—along with the support of the Streltsy (a prestigious arm of the Russian armed forces)—that managed to get both Ivan and Peter declared co-rulers. And, of course, Sophia herself was made regent over both of them. Sophia would remain regent for seven years.

During her stewardship, there were foreign policy successes, as well as failures. One of the most important foreign policy efforts the Russians achieved was reaching an agreement with China in 1689, which spelled out the territorial terms of the Far East between the two neighboring powers. Sophia fell short, however, when it came to dealing with a resurgence of Tatar might in Crimea, and after failing to put down Tatar raiding parties that were being launched from Russia's southern flanks, many became disenchanted with her leadership.

It was at this point that the members of the Streltsy, who had helped Sophia claw her way to power, began to turn on her. Sophia, in the meantime, soon came to accept that it was young Peter who would most likely become the ultimate ruler of Russia. Peter was now seventeen. He just married his first wife, Eudoxia Lopukhina, and made moves to begin his own court; he seemed poised to take on more of the trappings of a traditional tsar. It was for this reason that Sophia began to plot against her own half-brother.

Peter was raised in a suburb of Moscow outside of the palace; this made him fairly far removed from the intrigues afoot at the center of imperial power. But as Peter reached the age of his majority, he was alerted by disgruntled members of the Streltsy that Sophia was seeking to have him killed. Thanks to this heads-up, Peter was able to leave the palace before his would-be assassins arrived.

Shortly after his departure, a detachment of troops arrived at the palace searching for Peter. With the guards on duty at the palace apparently ignorant as to why a group of armed men would show up in the middle of the night, the intruders questioned the guards as to Peter's whereabouts. The guards flatly informed them that Peter had abruptly departed without informing them of where he was going.

After this squad of assassins realized that they had missed their prey, they simply turned around and made their way back to Sophia to report what they had learned. Peter, in the meantime, had made his way to a nearby monastery called the Monastery of the Trinity, which he used as a safe house to avoid his enemies. From here, he sent word back to Sophia that he was not only alive and well but also that he knew all about the plot she had concocted to end his life.

Sophia, for her part, adamantly denied being involved in any such plot, and she claimed that the troops that arrived at Peter's residence in the middle of the night were merely there to relieve the guard. As one might imagine, the notion that a whole detachment of troops would have to be sent to relieve a small contingent of palace guards struck anyone who heard it as being patently absurd.

Clinging to her flimsy excuses and attempts to cover up what had happened, Sophia began to lose support rapidly. Soon, notable officials were showing up at the monastery to swear their allegiance to Peter. The true strength of a tsar, however, remained in the hands of the Streltsy, and it was their favor that Peter needed in order to claw his way back to power.

In the meantime, Sophia had the sickly Tsar Ivan speak before an assembled troupe of the Streltsy and claim that it was Peter who was in the wrong and that Peter had holed up in a monastery with ill intentions in mind. In fact, it was claimed that he was plotting against the Russian state. Ivan—apparently speaking words fed to him by Sophia—then went on to state that he had heard reports that Peter was attempting to get the Streltsy to defect to his side.

Ivan declared that such actions would be considered treasonous and that any who attempted as much would face severe consequences. These harsh words, however, seemed to have the opposite effect. Disgusted members of the guard began to peel away one after the other, abandoning Ivan and joining up with Peter. Sophia realized that the Streltsy was abandoning her cause, and she began to panic.

Knowing that labeling Peter as an enemy of the state was not going to work for her, she then changed tack and attempted to broker peace with him instead. It is said that she sent a special envoy consisting of family members to the monastery where Peter was holed up, hoping that they would be able to negotiate a truce between them. Sophia wanted her relatives to present her as being innocent of any wrongdoing and to insist that the whole thing was really just a big misunderstanding.

However, the relatives would be convinced by Peter's own testimony that he truly had been wronged and that he truly did have to flee for his life because of Sophia's plot. The family members were so saddened at this realization that they vowed to not return to Moscow and instead stay by Peter's side at the monastery. Sophia soon learned of these happenings and became absolutely frantic.

To her, it seemed that practically the whole country had turned on her, and now she knew that she would be fighting not for power but her very survival. Treacherous actions such as hers, after all, were often punished by death. As such, Sophia played the only card she felt she had left in her dwindling deck. She reached out to the patriarch and requested that this respected religious leader work on her behalf and beseech Peter to have mercy on her.

The patriarch felt sorry for Sophia and agreed to do just as she asked. However, this effort would meet with abysmal failure as well. After the patriarch spoke with Peter, he, too, became quite convinced of Sophia's guilt. Not only that, Peter supposedly provided the holy man with evidence that if Sophia's efforts had been successful, she had plans to immediately remove the current patriarch in favor of her own preferred pick. Faced with such terrible realities, the patriarch decided to stay at the monastery with Peter rather than risk going back to the treacherous Sophia.

All of this resulted in the main orchestrators of the plot being tried and punished for their crimes against the empire. Most were either executed or sent off to live in exile in Siberia. As for the main architect, Sophia, Peter ended up showing restraint simply to avoid the scandal of having to punish a member of his own family. He opted to simply have her interred into a nunnery, where she would spend the rest of her life contemplating all of the tumult and distress that she had brought about.

With Sophia taken care of, the co-rulership of Ivan and Peter was restored. It seems that no one suspected Ivan of taking any direct part in the plot. It was believed that he was merely an unwitting pawn of Sophia's. So, when Peter made his grand entrance back to the palace in Moscow, he was greeted by his brother Ivan, who is said to have wished him well.

Although Ivan and Peter were supposed to be co-rulers, the true power lay in the hands of Peter and his ministers. This was apparently the only way it could have been since Ivan was still plagued with health problems and deemed too feeble to rule on his own. It has been said that rather than being bothered with matters of state, he spent most of his time in religious devotion. Some historians say he was merely getting himself ready for his own demise since his health was so precarious at the time. Regardless, Ivan would live on for another seven years before finally succumbing to his illness in 1696. This left Peter, then twenty-three years of age, the sole ruler of the empire.

As the sole ruler of the realm, one of Peter's biggest priorities was to make sure that Russia had a strong fighting force at its disposal. Early on in his reign, he made sure that the faltering navy was outfitted with more modern armaments and that it was ready to go on the offensive at a moment's notice. And in the summer of that year, a naval assault was launched against the Ottoman base in the city of Azov, which is situated on the Don River.

The fact that the Ottomans had a toehold in the region had been an eyesore for the Russians for some time, and Peter decided to finally do something about it. The city was successfully seized by the Russians, and the Ottomans were driven out. This strategically important fortress, which was located in the middle of the Don River, now gave the Russians a means of accessing the Black Sea.

Along with securing Russia's eastern frontier, Peter, who had been brought up in the suburbs of Moscow where there was a heavy presence of Western Europeans, such as Germans, French, and the like, was also keenly interested in Westernizing his fellow countrymen. Peter came to the conclusion that Russia needed to be a place where the East met the West and that Western learning could provide Russia with the shot to the arm it needed to remain a viable power.

Tsar Peter (who gave his name to Russia's westernmost metropolis—St. Petersburg) would indeed become known for establishing academies just as much as he was known for establishing armament factories. Peter very much desired for Russia to gain some of the enlightenment that he had experienced from European ex-pats during his youth in suburban Moscow.

Peter could be rather blunt in his prejudices over Western ways. He insisted his associates dress in Western clothes, and at one point, he even proposed a "beard tax" in order to get Russian men to start shaving off their beards! As one can imagine, for the hardline conformists to the old Russian ways and traditions, such things were not so easy to take. And in the long run, despite all of Peter's efforts, only a very small number of the elite within his own inner circle really took this Westernization to heart. Some of his inner circle attempted to conform just to please the tsar, but those on the periphery were just as adamant not to do so.

Of course, Peter had much more to worry about than the length of his ministers' beards, and by 1698, his main concern became what to do about the Streltsy. Members of the group had already plotted to launch a coup against him, and due to their grip on martial power, those who remained could never be entirely trusted. The group had become volatile and unpredictable.

And Peter could not contend with such an unpredictable force operating in his own backyard. He knew that he had to act, so, in the summer of 1698, after returning to Moscow from a trip abroad, he learned that certain factions within the Streltsy had plotted a rebellion. Peter immediately rounded up the architects behind the revolt and had them executed. He also had several others exiled to the newly incorporated territory in Siberia.

And Peter was not done just yet. He then took further action by having the entire Streltsy dismantled and removed from service. Once the home front was secure, Peter began to look toward some of the more daunting challenges that he faced abroad. First and foremost on his mind was the potential for a conflict with Sweden. Sweden was then in control of the Baltic Sea, and it had seized territory during the Russian Time of Troubles and denied Russia access ever since. In order for Russia to be able to make use of this body of water, they would have to go through Sweden to get it.

With Russian forces mobilized, hostilities then erupted in what would be called the Battle of Narva, which took place on November 30th, 1700. In this engagement, Peter's army proved to be too outdated to take on the finely tuned might of Sweden. The Russians were delivered a decisive defeat. Swedish King Charles XII proved to be a brilliant strategist. He utilized the weather, with his forces being sent storming into Russian troops in the middle of a blizzard. The Swedes were obscured in the torrential snowfall as they cut down Russian troops.

The Russians did not even know what hit them. The only thing that saved Peter's forces from complete annihilation was that Sweden became bogged down with additional fighting in Poland and had to redirect its forces to take on the Poles. By doing so, the Swedes failed to finish the Russian army off. Peter made full use of this distraction to regroup and rebuild his army. And by the following year, Peter's forces were back on the field. While the Swedes were partially distracted in Poland, Russian troops were able to seize a chunk of Swedish territory in the so-called "Ingermanland" or, as it was sometimes otherwise known, "Ingria."

Here, in Ingria, Peter the Great founded the city of St. Petersburg in 1703. The city was obviously named after Saint Peter, but it was no doubt a homage to Tsar Peter as well. Although Moscow remained the so-called third Rome in the eyes of most Russians, St. Petersburg was certainly an attractive alternative.

Besides city-building, much of Peter's resources remained focused on building up his military. At this time, Peter enacted a massive conscription of the regular populace into the army. In the meantime, the Swedes would manage to defeat Poland, and with the Poles put down in the west, the Swedes were able to turn their attention back to the Russians in the east.

The Swedish forces launched a major offensive against Russia in 1708. Sweden then scored a major victory in the Battle of Holowczyn (also called the Battle of Golovchin). King Charles of Sweden was able to successfully seize Grodno (today in western Belarus) from Peter and further established fortifications all along the Dnieper River.

Peter began to have other problems on his hands. The Russians resented being forced into conscription, and they began to grow increasingly discontented. Revolts in the frontier regions of the empire were not uncommon. For example, a major insurrection from the Bashkirs, a Turkic tribe, was not completely put down until 1709.

After the defeat at the Battle of Holowczyn, Peter was eventually able to cut his losses and recoup, leading the Russian troops to victory in the fall of 1708 in a battle near the settlement of Lesnaya. There, Russian troops not only managed to defeat a Swedish detachment but also took the Swedish supply train right along with it. This was a devastating blow for Sweden since it reduced its ability to restock its forces in the region.

Charles had been planning to march directly on Moscow, but with his supplies disrupted, this became an impossibility. Instead, the Swedes went on the defensive and prepared to regain the upper hand against the Russians by confronting them where they had regrouped in Ukraine. It was now a do-or-die situation for the Swedes, and they put everything on the table as they faced off against the Russians in the Battle of Poltava, which took place in central Ukraine in 1709. Peter was able to continue his momentum, and for once, the Russian army delivered a decisive defeat to Sweden.

At that time, Sweden had a population of just around two million people, and there was no way that it could continue waging war against the juggernaut of Russia, which seemed to have an endless supply of men and materiel for its armed forces. In Peter the Great's victory, his newly modernized artillery managed to play a decisive role in preventing the Swedes from coming back from the brink. In the aftermath of Sweden's defeat, Russia ended up controlling a territory that stretched from Riga to Vyborg. This means Russia practically had control over the entire expanse of the Baltic coast. They also now had considerable sway over Sweden. This was the moment that the Russian giant rose from being a junior partner to a major power in the Baltic region.

However, Peter ended up overplaying his hand. After learning that the Swedish monarch Charles, who had escaped annihilation in the Battle of Poltava, along with a small band of loyal followers, had sought refuge in the Ottoman Empire, he decided to seek his old foe out. This would lead to open hostilities between the Russians and Ottomans.

Exactly how this all played out is a little murky. Some accounts seem to suggest that Peter was the one who began battling the Ottomans, while others seem to indicate that Turkey began saber-rattling against Russia. At any rate, Peter used the presence of Charles in the Ottoman Empire as an excuse to launch a punitive expedition against the Ottomans.

This led to the Russo-Ottoman War, which began in 1710. Despite Peter's confidence that they would easily trounce the Ottomans, the campaign did not go very well for the Russians. Since the days of Western Europe's galvanized zealousness for crusades had long passed, Peter was hard-pressed to find any Western allies to support him. Instead, he sought to stir up rebellion among the Slavic and Greek peoples within the Ottoman Empire. He was hoping, for example, that the Ottoman-controlled Balkans might rise up to join the Russians against the Turks.

These overtures seemed to bear some fruit and resulted in auxiliary forces from Wallachia and Moldavia. Most importantly, however, the prince of Wallachia promised to provide the Russian army with supplies. But the prince fell through on his promise, and soon, the Russian forces had overextended themselves and were lacking proper provisions.

The Russian troops then made their way down the Pruth (Prut) River, only to end up completely encircled by a force of Ottoman Turks about 200,000 strong. Peter's men were in no shape to fight, and ultimately, Peter had to agree to back off. Peter then signed a humiliating truce with the Turks, which spared his troops from being massacred yet forced him to give back the previously won port of Azov. The only bright spot of the agreement was that the sultan agreed to expel the Swedish king, Charles XII, from his territory. Still, the disastrous results of Peter's Ottoman campaign put a dent in the people's perception of him as a military commander.

Nevertheless, Peter renewed his campaign against Sweden, and in 1714, the Russian fleet delivered a crushing blow to the Swedish fleet. The war dragged on over the next few years, and Sweden was ultimately forced to enter into peace talks in 1721. These efforts resulted in the Treaty of Nystad on August 30th, 1721, which stipulated that Russia would have full control of the Baltic regions of Estonia, Latvia, and Ingria. This was quite a boon for Russia since it secured control of the Baltic coast, as well as provided a bulwark of territories to buffer St. Petersburg from future hostilities.

As successful as Peter's later campaigns against Sweden were, his home life had been suffering for some time. Peter had divorced his first wife, Tsarina Eudoxia Lopukhina, in 1698. Prior to their parting, the tsarina had delivered an heir to the throne, a son named Alexei Petrovich. It is thought that Peter secretly married his second wife, a Polish-Lithuanian peasant by the name of Marta Helena Skowronska, in 1707. They officially married in 1712. You perhaps might know Marta by the name she adopted in 1705 when she converted to Orthodoxy: Catherine.

Peter and Catherine would have several children together, but all potential male heirs would end up preceding their father in death. The greatest tragedy of all, however, was in regard to Peter's eldest son, Alexei, from his first marriage.

It was suspected that Alexei had been plotting to overthrow his father. When Alexei received word that he was under suspicion of launching a coup, he fled the country. Peter and his advisors were now worried that a foreign adversary might exploit the situation and make Alexei their pawn. Peter's government managed to convince Alexei to return, feigning that all would be forgiven. This was not the case, however, and as soon as Alexei arrived back in Russia, he was promptly thrown behind bars. Peter showed no mercy to his own son, as he had Alexei tried and sentenced to death.

Alexei is said to have perished from a mixture of shock and the generally dreadful conditions of his confinement before his execution day even arrived. He was only twenty-eight years old at the time. One could easily argue that since Peter the Great had his own son killed that he was capable of a ruthlessness on par with Ivan the Terrible. You could maybe even argue that Peter was more terrible than Tsar Ivan IV in this regard since Ivan killed his son in a moment of rage, whereas Peter killed his son with cold, calculated reason.

At any rate, with the death of his eldest son, Peter was left without an heir, and by the time of his death, all of his potential male heirs with his second wife had perished from childhood maladies—a phenomenon that was all too common at the time. Peter himself would then succumb to a series of health complications, passing away on February 8th, 1725. Although Catherine would rule in her husband's place through a council of court ministers until her own death in 1727, the line of succession then fell upon Peter's grandson—the son of the deceased Alexei—Peter II.

Peter II was only twelve years old at the time, and he would be stewarded by a regency council. However, Peter II ended up perishing due to smallpox in 1730 before he could even be officially crowned. After his untimely death, the Supreme Privy Council took it upon themselves to select Peter's niece, Anna of Courland, to serve as empress. This would only be done, however, if certain conditions were met. Among the terms of the agreement was that Anna would not be able to declare war without the consent of the council.

This was a major change in the Russian government, which up until that point had been run as an absolute monarchy. In the past, whatever the tsar ordered was done, and it was done without question. And nothing short of a successful coup or full-scale revolution would change the orders issued by a sitting tsar. The council also demanded that Anna consult them before raising taxes or making adjustments to the empire's revenue. They also insisted on getting a chance to influence all of her important appointments to the state governing apparatus.

In some ways, limiting the power of the Russian monarch seemed to be a move toward a constitutional monarchy, such as England. But in this case, it was really more of a transitioning toward an oligarchy—the rule of an elite few who pulled the strings of the empress. At any rate, the Supreme Privy Council's ability to curtail the power of the imperial monarch would prove to be entirely short-lived.

Upon coming to power, Anna proved herself to be a quite able stateswoman, and she managed to maneuver factions who were discontent with the nobles—primarily officers in the military—to her side. Soon enough, the odds were stacked against the nobles, and they were forced to take back their conditions, which allowed the imperial throne to once again be the sole ruling force of Russia. Anna would reign for ten more years, passing away in 1740.

One of the most pivotal instances during that ten-year span was the discovery of Alaska. The Russians had the idea that the American continent was in between Western Europe and their most eastern territory, but where the closest point of the North American continent was, in relation to Russia, had yet to be determined. In 1732, Russian explorer Ivan Fyodorov figured it out by making landfall in what he termed the "Great Land," which, as it turns out, is what today we call Alaska. This initial foray into Alaska would then be followed by the expeditions of Captain Vitus Bering (for whom the Bering Strait is named) and Captain Aleksei Chirkov in 1741.

At any rate, after Elizabeth's passing, the imperial crown was then given to her great-nephew, Ivan VI, who ruled for a very short time before he was arrested during a coup in January of 1742. Russian insiders were able to put Elizabeth, the daughter of Peter the Great, on the throne. Elizabeth would be one of the longer-lived monarchs of Peter the Great's immediate successors, as she went on to reign for twenty years.

The most notable event of Elizabeth's reign was the Seven Years' War, which was being waged in Europe against Prussia at the time. Prussia was primarily made up of territories in modern-day Germany, but it also contained sections of modern-day Belgium, Denmark, and even Russia.

The Seven Years' War was a rather complicated affair. The foundations for this global conflict were actually laid in what was known as the French and Indian War. Although the title of the aforementioned conflict might be a confusing one, the French and Indian War was not a war between Native Americans and French forces. On the contrary, it was called that because it was a war waged between French forces in North America and their Native American allies against the British. Prussia was allied with Britain at the time, whereas Prussia's mortal enemy, Austria, was aligned with France.

After the outbreak of open hostilities between the British and the French, Prussia took the initiative and took on the Austrians. At the outset, Russia sided with Austria and began to engage the Prussians militarily. Initially, the Russians seemed to have the upper hand, and East Prussia was successfully seized by the Russian military under the guidance of Russian General Count Pyotr (Peter) Saltykov. Saltykov's forces eventually marched all the way to Berlin.

In 1762, the abrupt passing of Empress Elizabeth took this military victory and turned it into a political defeat. The tsar who took Elizbeth's place—Peter III—sympathized with the Prussians. Just as Russia was on the verge of absolute victory, he did the unthinkable—he negotiated a peace treaty.

As one might imagine, the military generals, who had been so successful on the field of war, were deeply dismayed that they were being forced to give up all of their gains due to the ill-conceived political meanderings of their commander-in-chief. This frustration eventually erupted into the so-called "Officer's Revolt," which resulted in Peter III's overthrow and the placement of his own wife, Catherine (also known as Catherine the Great), on the throne in his place.

Chapter 4 – Catherine the Great

"In politics a capable ruler must be guided by circumstances, conjectures and conjunctions."

-Catherine the Great

It was a coup that stunned the world. Tsar Peter III of Russia had been overthrown by his own wife. Catherine the Great, of course, could not take sole credit for the machinations since there was a whole cadre of disaffected military officers behind her. Outsiders obviously had many questions about this coup. First of all, how could a wife betray her husband in such a manner?

Catherine and Peter III's marriage was described as a loveless one. It was, in fact, an arranged marriage. Catherine was of German heritage and hailed from Prussia. The marriage had originally been engineered by Empress Elizabeth's top advisor Count Lestocq and Frederick the Great of Prussia as a means of strengthening Russo-Prussian relations.

Once married, however, whatever attraction Catherine may have initially had for Peter III quickly disappeared. The two began to essentially live like strangers in the same imperial palace. They both had extramarital affairs and were really only husband and wife in name only. Even the son that Catherine and Peter III supposedly had together during their short marriage—Paul I—has long been suspected of being a product of Catherine and one of her lovers rather than being the offspring of Peter III.

At any rate, when Empress Elizabeth passed on January 5th, 1762, Peter III became tsar, and Catherine became the tsarina. As mentioned in the previous chapter, by this time, Russia was embroiled in the Seven Years' War. And despite the fact that the tsar was married to a woman who originally hailed from Prussia, the Russians and Prussians were at each other's throats when Peter III came to the throne. At the time of Peter III's coronation, Russia had gained the upper hand.

It was for this reason that it came as such a shock when Peter III began to scale back the Russian offensive, handing Prussia a victory that should have been a defeat. It was not long before enraged Russian ministers of state turned on Peter III for his reversal of course in the war with Prussia. This frustration then metastasized in an all-out coup against Peter III known as the "Officer's Revolt." Catherine herself latched onto the opportunity as a means to get rid of her unwanted husband.

The fact that Catherine, a Prussian woman of German origin, could get the people to side with her to overthrow a Russian-born monarch is quite incredible. This serves as a testament to how unpopular Peter III and his policies had become. And it was with this backdrop of dissatisfaction with the previous regime that Catherine was coronated as empress on September 22nd, 1762.

In her first few years on the throne, Catherine seemed to have developed a strong fear of the very elements that brought her to power: the officer class. As such, she slowly sought to limit their power, and at the same time, she increased the centralized authority of the sitting monarch. These efforts led to the creation of a special commission in 1767 referred to as the "Catherine's Law Code Commission."

This group, which was tasked with sorting out the exact nature of just what the Russian social compact would be, first met in July of 1767. The commission body was made up primarily of nobles, local officials, Cossacks, and the odnodvortsy, the latter of whom were descendants of the militarized peasants who had manned the frontier lines. The members were supposed to find common ground, but such things were, of course, much easier said than done.

And soon after the council began hammering out the new legal code, developments on the international stage would greatly hamper their progress.

In an attempt to assert her will, Catherine involved Russia with the internal affairs of Poland. The Polish state had been eyed by Russia for a long time, and Catherine decided to try her hand at peeling away territory from the Poles. Russian agents stirred discord among the Poles by sponsoring legislation beneficial to the Orthodox and Protestant minorities of this staunchly Catholic country.

Resentment of these developments led to the outbreak of military conflict in 1768 in what would become known as the War of the Bar Confederation. In this war, a group of Polish elites led an armed uprising against the Russians at Poland's Bar Fortress, located in the town of Podolia.

And while Russian troops were being mobilized to take on the threat posed by Poland, the Ottoman Empire suddenly took advantage of this distraction and launched a surprise attack on Russian possessions, laying siege to the Caucasus and Crimea. This led to Catherine declaring war on the Ottoman Turks in 1768.

The Russian people proved to be very enthusiastic in fighting off the Turks, and many signed on for what was viewed as a patriotic cause. At that time, the Russian armed forces were being led by Russian General Count Pyotr Rumyantsev. The Russian army was sent down the Danube as a naval squadron was summoned out of the Baltic Sea.

This naval group had the daunting task of exiting out of the Black Sea in the north and then going all the way around Western Europe and into the Mediterranean to engage the Ottomans on the opposite side. This two-pronged approach proved highly successful for the Russians. And by 1770, the Ottomans were suffering terrible defeats. Turkish ships were being literally blown out of the water while Russian infantry marched on Ottoman territory.

The only real failure the Russian faced was in their attempt to instigate an uprising of the Greek population under Ottoman occupation. The Greeks attempted to rise up against their Ottoman overlords, but they were ultimately put down by the Ottomans, who did not hesitate to slaughter the Greeks wholesale. Even a Russian infantry group that attempted landings on the Greek mainland was ultimately beaten back.

This was, of course, prior to Greece's independence from Ottoman rule, and there was much talk of the Russians perhaps ripping Greece from the Ottoman grip. But at this time, such a task proved to be too much for the Russians to handle. The Russo-Turkish War would rage on until 1774; it would not come to a close until the Treaty of Kuchuk Kainarji was signed.

According to the terms of this treaty, the mouths of the Bug and Dnieper Rivers were granted to the Russians, along with the estuary of the Don River and the Kerch Strait in the Black Sea. The Ottomans also promised to protect Christians and their churches that were under their dominion.

The idea that a Christian power—especially an Orthodox power—was eliciting such pledges from the Ottomans was inspiring for Greek Orthodox Christians in Greece and other Greek-speaking regions. Ever since the Greek-oriented Byzantine Empire had collapsed. Greek Orthodox Christians were largely on their own. Having the Orthodox Christian power of Russia back them up like this was a big deal to oppressed Greeks in the region, even if, in reality, the Ottomans did not always abide by their pledge.

At the end of this conflict, Russia agreed to a few concessions of its own. First of all, the Russians conceded Wallachia and Moldavia, which were regions in the Balkans that had previously been run by the Ottomans, back to the Ottoman Empire after seizing them during the war.

However, it would not be long before relations between the Russians and the Ottomans would deteriorate. After conflict broke out in the Crimea region in 1783, the Ottomans slowly became pulled into another war with Russia, a war that would be officially declared in 1787.

During this latest go-round with the Ottomans, another old Russian nemesis—Sweden—decided to take on the distracted Russians; it declared war on Russia the following year. Soon thereafter, yet another Russian enemy came out of the woodwork when Prussia followed Sweden's lead and prepared for war against Russia as well. At this point, Russia was literally encircled by hostile camps.

You might think that this would be an occasion for a leader of such a beleaguered nation to panic, but Empress Catherine managed to prove her steely nerves and remained a steady hand at the helm. Under her guidance, the Russian Navy was able to make short work of Sweden, destroying Swedish craft as they approached St. Petersburg. This victory was followed by a Russian invasion of Turkish holdings down the Danube in 1789.

Prussia, in the meantime, quickly became distracted by the outbreak of the French Revolution, and it dropped out of the conflict. In the end, Russia managed to repel all of its enemies and forced the Ottomans to sue for peace in 1792. Yes, despite the sometimes scandalous nature of her personal life, Catherine's prowess as a leader really did make her great.

But there was one foe that even this daring and bold monarch could not defeat—the passage of time. Catherine, for all of her strength, was getting older, and her health was going into decline.

Catherine the Great would abruptly perish a few years later, dying from a stroke in 1796.

Chapter 5 – From Tsar Paul I to Tsar Alexander I

"He who has talent in him must be purer in soul than anyone else. Another will be forgiven much, but to him it will not be forgiven. A man who leaves the house in bright, festive clothes needs only one drop of mud splashed from under a wheel, and people all surround him, point their fingers at him, and talk about his slovenliness, while the same people ignore many spots on other passers-by who are wearing everyday clothes. For on everyday clothes the spots do not show."

-Nikolai Gogol

After the passing of Catherine the Great in 1796, the stewardship of Russia was taken over by her son, Paul I. Just like his father, the mental state of Paul would often be called into question. And if certain anecdotes are to be believed, it was the very day after his mother's death that some of Paul's most acute madness was exhibited.

According to one account, he actually had his father (alleged father anyway) Peter III's skeleton exhumed and his remains placed upon the imperial throne. This macabre act was supposedly carried out in order to demonstrate the legitimacy of his own succession.

Paul's time on the throne would ultimately be short-lived, spanning from 1796 to 1801. But the time in which he reigned was still a pivotal one, as he had to deal with the aftermath of the French Revolution and the rise of Napoleon, as well as the influx of the Western intellectualism of the day. Paul, for his part, was drawn to Western advancements and wished to reform Russia along Western lines. However, Paul was often unstable in temperament, which led to instability in his brief reign.

As it pertains to Napoleonic France, Paul was indeed successful in joining the growing alliance against France. In 1798, Russia even found itself aligned with its old enemy, the Ottoman Turks, as Russia, the Ottoman Empire, England, Austria, and the Kingdom of Naples all joined forces to thwart the aggressive advance of French conquest that was occurring at the time.

That very year, General Napoleon Bonaparte led French forces into Egypt on a mad scheme to cut off British supply lines and break into British-controlled India. The Russians and the Turks, in the meantime, colluded together to send a joint squadron of naval craft through the Adriatic to take on the French.

The French were ultimately driven out of their holdings on the Ionian Islands. Paul also established another interesting foothold for Russia by making contact with the Knights of Malta. The Knights of Malta were holdouts from the Crusades—formerly the Knights Hospitaller—who had been holed up on the island, working to repel Turkish attacks from pirates for several centuries. Napoleon Bonaparte brought the reign of the Knights of Malta to an end when French forces invaded the island in 1798. Survivors sought refuge in Russia, and none other than Tsar Paul I became the next grandmaster of the order. Paul felt that being able to claim leadership of such an esteemed order would help him gain inroads with the heads of state of Europe, but it really only served to add to his eccentricities.

The following year, Tsar Paul sent a force of Russians to take on the main contingent of French forces in Austria. The battle then moved to Italy, where the French were defeated. The Russian forces were on the verge of invading France proper, but the tsar decided to mobilize forces in Switzerland to remove the remaining French troops there that were threatening Austria. This was done apparently at Austria's request.

Paul soon grew weary of being a plaything of the foreign powers, and he began to question his alliances. Paul decided better of it all and washed his hands of the whole thing, concluding a separate peace agreement with France. This agreement did not affect relations with Russia's newfound ally of the Ottoman Turks, but it did turn the British against Russia. And when Britain turned on Russia, Paul seems to have had a bit of a mental slip.

Paul's first course of action was reasonable enough; he ordered an embargo on England. But his next set of instructions were absolutely bewildering. He ordered Russian forces to march on British-controlled India. The Russian forces that were sent for this impossible task were not even equipped with adequate maps to reach the Indian subcontinent, and it is said that they lost half their horses in the desert of the Russian frontier just trying to leave Russia.

This bizarre and fruitless campaign turned the Russian state against its ruler, and soon, plots were under way to have the tsar killed. And on March 24th, 1801, Emperor Paul I was indeed assassinated. A group of disgruntled military officers stormed into the tsar's bedchamber and found him hiding behind a curtain. They grabbed the ruler and forced him to sign his abdication. When Paul refused, they squeezed the life right out of him. After strangling him, they then stomped on his corpse for good measure to make sure that he was dead.

Paul was succeeded by his eldest son, Alexander, who at the time was twenty-three years old. Before Paul's death, Tsar Alexander had been approached by the military officers who had his father killed, and Alexander agreed with having his father removed from power. However, Alexander would always insist that he did not think the officers would actually kill his father. He figured they would simply have him arrested and removed from power. Alexander was shocked to learn what actually happened to his dad, and he would harbor much guilt over the ordeal for the rest of his life.

At any rate, Alexander proved to be a much more able statesman and politician than his father. Alexander is said to have been extremely charismatic, and he had an uncanny ability of coming up with ideas and then convincing his ministers that they were actually their ideas. It has been said that whenever he wanted to move policy in a certain direction, he would casually mention the factors involved around his ministers in such an offhand manner that it was almost as if he were planting subliminal messages.

And then, when one of his ministers half-recalled certain remarks and made mention of them, Alexander would essentially slap them on the back and congratulate them, saying, "Well, that's a great idea!" By tricking his ministers into thinking that they were the ones coming up with these ideas, Alexander was able to prevent disagreement on policy issues. Interestingly enough, it also allowed him to freely blame them if something were to go awry.

Alexander was a popular ruler from the very beginning. It certainly was helpful that his greatly disliked father Paul had set the bar fairly low, but Alexander proved that he could be a popular leader by virtue of his own qualities of leadership. Early on in his reign, he began to rein in the more draconian measures of his predecessors by issuing long-lasting reforms.

He reformed the police, making sure that what had previously been routine torture sessions of suspected criminals while in police custody were abolished and that the rights of the accused were respected. He also reformed land ownership, making it easier for an individual to gain deeds to properties. Sadly, this did not help the serfs, who were still basically bondservants to the plots of their landlords.

However, Alexander received some pushback from the Russian elite; in particular, the nobles petitioned him to fill up the Russian Senate with their ranks. Alexander did indeed reform the Senate in 1802, but he did not heed the demands of the elite. He also allowed the Senate to have the ability to criticize and argue against his executive orders.

One of Alexander's most important executive decisions involved the so-called "free landowners." He issued an order on March 4th, 1803, which attempted to provide a path for freedom for the countless serfs who were bonded to the land of the landlords for whom they labored.

Further domestic reform had to be put on hold, however, as Napoleonic France once again posed a challenge to the world. In 1805, Russia found itself once again aligned with Britain and Austria so they could take on the French menace.

French forces had already delivered a decisive blow to the Austrians at the Battle of Ulm, which took place around the German town of the same name on October 16th, 1805. Here, the French Army managed to smash right through the Austrian lines and took a large contingent of Austrian troops prisoner. It now appeared that the French were on the verge of taking Vienna itself. It was for this reason that Austria banged on the door of its ally Russia and had Russian troops join together with what remained of the Austrian military to take on the French threat.

With the backup of the Russians, this unified force outnumbered Napoleon's army, and they should have been able to make short work of Napoleon, who had crowned himself emperor of France in 1804. But in one of the greatest feats in history, Napoleon would prove just how cunning of a military commander he was. Right when it seemed that Napoleon was about to be cornered and defeated, he pretended to surrender. However, this was only a means for buying time, and during the temporary lull in fighting, he managed to evacuate his entire army.

As the French fled, the Russian forces were in hot pursuit, and they appeared ready to make short work of them. Napoleon, however, led them right over a frozen river—the Austerlitz River. The French made it across first and then turned their artillery on both the Russian troops and the frozen ice. It was not long before the ice buckled, and an entire Russian regiment fell to its watery death. This was the massacre that would become known as the Battle of Austerlitz.

With their Russian allies incapacitated, Austria was forced to enter into a peace deal with Napoleon called the Peace of Pressburg. However, Russian forces would rally once again, and they would take on Napoleon in Poland in 1807. This battle was a struggle for both sides, but after heavy casualties for both the French and the Russians, the French were eventually able to gain the upper hand.

It was the Battle of Friedland, which followed, however, which made the French the clear victors. In the bloody carnage of this battle, over twenty thousand Russians perished. Due to such shocking losses, Alexander was forced to sue for peace, and on June 25th, 1807, he met Napoleon Bonaparte face to face. Truth be told, Alexander admired Napoleon, both for his military genius and his liberal social views. Napoleon, for his part, was endearing to Alexander to his face, but behind his back, Napoleon was always quick to poke fun at the tsar, reminding anyone and everyone within earshot of the notion that Alexander had his own father killed.

At any rate, the two men managed to hammer out the Treaty of Tilsit, which would temporarily end hostilities between the two nations. Another interesting effect of the treaty was that Alexander ordered the Russian Orthodox Church to take back their previous pronouncements that Napoleon was the antichrist.

The most important aspect of the treaty was the stipulation insisted by Napoleon that Russia refuse to conduct trade with Britain. This was all a part of Napoleon's Continental System scheme, in which he wished to control the trade of the entire European continent and prevent his British enemies from having access to it. Alexander would break this agreement in 1811 when he went ahead and began to conduct trade with the British regardless.

The treaty with France was incredibly unpopular with the Russian people from the beginning, and when scarce commodities became tenfold what they normally would be, Russians were ready to take to the streets in protest. Lest he ended up assassinated like his father, Alexander decided he would be better off taking his chances on Napoleon's wrath and restarting trade with the British.

Of course, Napoleon was not happy about this. On June 22nd, 1812, he sent hundreds of thousands of troops to invade Russia. The French initially met little to no resistance. They stormed into the western frontiers of Russia to find them virtually abandoned.

At this time, the Russian military was suffering from severe setbacks and delays, and the incredibly unprepared Russian General Barclay de Tolly was wasting precious time getting the affairs of the Russian army in order. Alexander was sick of the general's negligence, so he had him sacked and put Mikhail Kutuzov in his place. Kutuzov had actually participated in the Battle of Austerlitz, and he was eager for revenge. And rather than chasing Napoleon, as the Russians had done in Austerlitz, he was determined to force Napoleon to come to him.

Kutuzov wanted to make the French dictator strain his troops to the limit before Kutuzov unleashed the full might of the Russian army against them. He also made sure to burn everything in Napoleon's path so that the French troops would not be able to live off the land. By utilizing a scorched-earth strategy, nothing was left for Napoleon. Even when the French made their way to Moscow on September 13th, 1812, they found it desolated and empty of all citizens, save for the poor dregs of society who were unable to be evacuated.

Nevertheless, Napoleon attempted to seize hold of the ashes of Moscow and claim victory. The Russian army under General Mikhail Kutuzov, in the meantime, had moved farther east, still waiting for just the right moment to strike. Unable to wait out the Russians any longer, Napoleon sent his forces east to engage them in October of 1812. At this point, the French Army had been severely weakened by sickness and lack of food, just as Mikhail had hoped they would be.

The Russians were able to make short work of this beleaguered and weary French force. The French forces buckled and attempted to make a tactical withdraw, but the Russians were once again in pursuit, and this time, there would be no frozen river to save the fleeing French. The Russians were able to systematically slaughter the French troops as they ran. Russia would then go on to lead a renewed allied push against the French, whose combined forces stormed Paris in 1814. Napoleon would then be exiled to an island prison in Elba.

However, Napoleon had one more daring chapter to write, as he escaped from his prison, returned to France, and started another war against Europe. The carnage would only end when the British managed to decisively defeat the French at the Battle of Waterloo in 1815. In the aftermath of Napoleon's final defeat, Alexander was at his peak. It seems that he had achieved what he always wanted—the forging of a strong international coalition of European powers.

But Alexander would prove more hamstrung by this arrangement than being a beneficiary of it. For example, when the Greek War of Independence broke out in 1821, which allowed the Greeks to finally shake off the Ottoman yoke once and for all, Russia was forced to sit on the sidelines. Even though the Greeks naturally looked toward the Russians as their big Orthodox brothers, Alexander was convinced by his European colleagues to stay out of it.

Many Russians were upset with this decision; they saw it as a missed opportunity to support the Orthodox faith. The Russians had long viewed themselves as the inheritors of Byzantium, yet when the Greek remnants of the old Byzantine Empire were rising up to throw off their conquerors, Russia would not get officially involved. This was a huge disappointment for many.

However, during the lead-up to the Greek Revolution, the Russians had been heavily involved behind the scenes, and as far back as 1812, they had meddled in Greek affairs. In 1812, the Russians sided with a rebellious provincial governor of the Ottomans named Ali Pasha, who promised the Russians that he would treat the Greeks well, reduce taxes, and get rid of forced labor. The Ottoman Empire was at war with this province, yet Russia made the bold move of voicing support.

As agitating as this was to the Ottomans, Russia initially was not willing to rock the boat beyond stating their support. But after the British began to get involved in the Greek Revolution in 1823—at least on a diplomatic level—and in light of widespread reports of Turkish atrocities, Russia began to reconsider its position. These developments would ultimately lead to the leading nations of Europe coming together to sign the Treaty of London in 1827. In this treaty, the signatories demanded that the Turks recognize Greece as an independent nation.

Of course, the Ottoman Turks refused to do so. This forced the European powers into a showdown with the Turks on October 20th, 1827, in which the Ottoman Empire was delivered a decisive defeat at the Battle of Navarino. It was truly a terrible blow to the Turks, as their aging and obsolete ships were literally blown out of the water by their adversaries. Shortly thereafter, the next Russo-Turkish War erupted, and it would take up much of 1828 and 1829.

Due to all of these developments, Greek independence was ultimately ensured. Although Tsar Alexander I helped to set them in motion, he did not live to see these final developments play out. Alexander had actually passed away on December 1st, 1825 (although some sources say November 19th), at the age of forty-seven. His successor, Nicholas I (Alexander's younger brother), would oversee the final stages of Greek independence.

Chapter 6 – Tsar Nicholas I and the Beginning of Alexander II's Reign

"Patriotism in its simplest, clearest, and most indubitable meaning is nothing but an instrument for the attainment of the government's ambitious and mercenary aims, and a renunciation of human dignity, common sense, and conscience by the governed, and a slavish submission to those who hold power. That is what is really preached wherever patriotism is championed. Patriotism is slavery."

-Leo Tolstoy

Nicholas had been sworn in as emperor on the day after Christmas—December 26th, 1825, to be exact. Shortly after he was sworn in, the Decembrist Revolt took place, in which some five hundred military officers attempted to force major reforms on Russia. The military officers wanted to institute a constitutional monarchy and move away from the highly centralized autocratic regime of the past. And instead of supporting Nicholas, they vied for an alternative tsar in the form of the former Tsar Alexander's uncle, Constantine.

In fact, even though Constantine had consciously refused to be a contender for the throne, the Decembrists made the false claim that Constantine had been denied the throne. They further claimed that Constantine was denied the chance to be tsar because he championed the institution of a constitutional monarchy, which was yet another false claim. But hey—who's counting? These agitators were determined to make Constantine their mouthpiece whether he agreed to it or not.

And continuing on with their fabricated fantasy, they then laid it on real thick by insisting that if Constantine was allowed to become emperor, he would raise the pay of any soldier who joined the cause! Perhaps the easiest way to dismiss this false narrative would have been for Constantine to show up in the Red Square himself and have him denounce the rabble-rousers as a bunch of liars and opportunists. But since Constantine was apparently not up for this task, Tsar Nicholas had the troops come in with artillery blazing instead.

Russian soldiers opened fire on the agitators, and after a large number of them were killed, the survivors fled the scene and forgot all about their aspirations for Constantine and their constitutional monarchy. Nicholas felt terrible for having to resort to violence against his own people so soon after coming to power, but he apparently felt that he had no choice. He had to gain control of a chaotic situation, and he had to gain control of it quickly.

To be sure, the Decembrists were not innocent of bloodshed; they had actually already assassinated a Russian general (who was also the military governor of St. Petersburg) named Miloradovich simply for approaching them to try and talk and deescalate the situation. Miloradovich came to the Decembrists with the best of intentions, and he was gunned down in cold blood. Nicholas, therefore, felt he had to come down hard in order to prevent all-out chaos from breaking loose.

In the aftermath of the Decembrist Revolt, 120 people were arrested and put on trial. Of these condemned men, five received the death penalty, but the vast majority were simply exiled to Siberia. Although Nicholas was dishing out the punishments, he sympathized with the agitators.

In order to come to grips with the angst that had led to this unrest, he launched a commission to investigate the root causes of the disturbance. Leading this commission was a man whose name comes down to us as A. D. Borovkov. Borovkov's conclusions were thought-provoking. He summarized his findings by stating, "The government itself had nourished the youth on free-thinking as on mother's milk." But even though this free thought had been encouraged, Borovkov stated that the fruits of it had been denied, thus resulting in agitation. In other words, the Russian youth were being educated to learn of all of the failings of Russian society yet were made entirely hopeless at the realization that they had not been given the tools to fix it.

Borovkov therefore concluded, "It is necessary to grant clear positive laws, to implant justice by introducing speedy legal procedures, to raise the moral education of the clergy, to strengthen the nobility, which has fallen into decay, ruined by loans in credit institutions, revive trade and industry by unshakable charters, improve the position of the cultivators of the soil, stop the humiliating sale of human beings, resurrect the fleet and encourage private people to take up sea-going...in a word to correct countless failings and abuses."

Although Nicholas was not ready for wholesale reform, he was aware that he needed to address some of the root causes that this commission found as being the factors before the chaos of the Decembrist Revolt. He noted the "confusion" of the agitators and decided to set down a new code of laws. This was an epic project that sought to codify and make universal all legal practices of the realm, a feat that was not completed until 1832. This was the first codification of Russian law in its entirety.

Before Nicholas established these universal statutes, laws and the consequences of breaking them could greatly vary from one part of the empire to another. Thanks to Nicholas, Russia's justice system began to operate on a more even keel. The most glaring problem of Russian society, of course, remained the forced labor of the serfs. Serfdom was essentially slavery in all but name, and many in Russia knew that it was nigh time for serfdom to be abolished.

But Nicholas, like his predecessors, preferred a more gradual approach to limiting and then ultimately getting rid of serfdom, lest he bring the wrath of the landlords down upon him. Nicholas, like so many others, wanted to get rid of the horrid practice, but he was not brave enough to do so. When he presided over the State Council in 1842, he described his exact feelings on the matter, saying, "There is no doubt that serfdom, in its present form, is an evil obvious to all; but to touch it now would of course be an even more ruinous evil."

Despite his dithering on serfdom, Nicholas did indeed take some of the Decembrists' criticisms seriously and set out to make reforms to at least meet them halfway. But at the same time, he also increased the power of the autocracy and instituted greater surveillance of activists, lest another Decembrist-styled revolt took place. Besides the threat of internal strife, Nicholas also had an external conflict on the horizon.

As mentioned in the previous chapter, Tsar Alexander I led the nation down the course of supporting Greek independence shortly before his death, and Nicholas continued the policy. This support of the Greek cause would lead to the outbreak of the Russo-Turkish War of 1828–1829.

Yes, yet another Russo-Turkish war was to be fought, and this one would have incredible consequences. The war was a slow slog at first, largely tied down in the Balkans, but the Russians managed to finally defeat a large Ottoman contingent at the town of Kulevcha. This forced the Turks to agree to a peace agreement at Adrianople, where they signed the Treaty of Adrianople. This latest victory against the

Turks was a boon for the Russians since the treaty granted them control of the mouth of the Danube and strengthened the overall Russian position on the Black Sea.

In addition to all of this, the independence of Greece was basically enshrined in stone. The Treaty of London in 1827 began the official recognition of Greek independence, but the Russian victories against the Ottomans in the Russo-Turkish War of 1828–1829 sealed the deal. The war also had the consequence of freeing up the Balkan states of Serbia, Moldavia, and Wallachia.

Russia did not have too long to bask in the glory of their triumph with the Ottomans before they were beset with new problems in foreign policy. Just a few years later, in 1831, a major uprising occurred in Russian-controlled Poland, forcing imperial troops to be sent in to put down the unrest. This led to many Poles fleeing as refugees, including one young Polish pianist who would become quite famous as an exiled ex-pat—Frederick Chopin.

After putting down the Polish uprising, further foreign policy problems would occur for Russia when the French Revolution of 1848 broke out. The new regime of Napoleon III decided to ingratiate itself with the Ottoman sultan and gain special privileges for French Catholics in Israel/Palestine. This resulted in the sultan confiscating the "keys to the Church of Bethlehem" from the Orthodox faithful in the region and then handing them over to the Catholics.

It may not seem like a big deal to us today, but in a time when people lived and breathed religion, it was deeply upsetting. This perhaps might go doubly for the Russians since they were viewed as the stewards of the Orthodox faith and even had an agreement with the Turks going way back, which accorded certain rights and privileges to the Orthodox faithful under Ottoman dominion. In order to challenge the Turks on this issue, Russian soldiers were stationed in Wallachia and Moldavia.

The Turks did not take too kindly to these threats. Rather than caving to the pressure, the Ottoman Empire ended up declaring war on the Russian Empire in 1853. At first, the Ottomans seemed like they were going to be destroyed by the Russians, as the Russians delivered a devastating blow to the Turkish fleet in the first phase of the war.

But then England and France joined the war, siding with the Ottomans against Russia. This changed everything. Although the Russians were able to take on the so-called "sick man of Europe"—in this case, the faltering Ottoman Empire—the combined might of England and France was much more than the Russian tsar had bargained for. And as if that was not bad enough, Austria then weighed in and gave Russia an ultimatum—leave Wallachia and Moldavia or else!

Russia was not willing to call Austria's bluff, and as a result, the Russian army stood down. But even so, the war was not over; it just entered a new phase, which would come to be known as the Crimean War. Russia was now on the defensive, and in the fall of 1854, a French and British combined navy besieged the Russian port of Sevastopol. As this drama was still unfolding, Tsar Nicholas I abruptly perished during the following spring, on March 2nd, 1855.

Bereft of its steady hand at the helm, by the fall of 1855, the Russians were forced to evacuate Fort Sevastopol. However, the Russians were more successful against the Ottomans, and after taking the Ottoman fort of Kars, they were able to force all parties to the table for peace talks. As a result, the Treaty of Paris was forged in 1856, ending the conflict between all parties.

But the deal that was hammered out was not too favorable for Russia. It allowed Russia to swap Sevastopol for Kars, but it also forced the Russians to limit their naval presence in the Black Sea. Russia also lost the southernmost portion of Bessarabia, with it being ceded to Moldavia. This prevented Russia from using the Danube. But perhaps the most troubling blow to Russian prestige was an ideological one, for Russia was forced to renounce all claims of authority over the affairs of the Orthodox faithful under Ottoman dominion. As this was the main reason for the war in the first place, Russia obviously lost face in this debacle.

After Nicholas's death in 1855, he was succeeded by his son, who became Alexander II. Tsar Alexander II came onto the throne knowing that Russia needed some pretty serious reforms. It is said that his father Nicholas even told him as much on his deathbed, as he apparently bluntly stated, "I am handing you command of the country in a poor state." The military needed retuning, the economy was faltering, and international prestige had been lost. But Alexander II knew that he had an even more pressing problem—the serfs.

In a world where forced labor was now viewed as the ultimate evil, the fact that Russia had a whole class of people called serfs, who had no control over their destiny and were entirely beholden to their landlords, was not only a moral evil but also added to the perception that Russia was culturally backward. Shortly into his reign, Alexander II indicated his willingness to tackle the problem by holding a meeting among the Russian elite to have an earnest discussion of what to do.

Rather than fearing a backlash, Alexander II honestly spoke with them of their own need to take immediate action. Alexander explained that "the existing system of serf-owning cannot remain unchanged. It is better to begin abolishing serfdom from above than to wait for it to begin to abolish itself from below. I ask you, gentlemen, to think of ways of doing this. Pass on my words to the nobles for consideration."

In this frank discussion, Alexander made the elite class realize that as much as they were afraid to shake up the status quo, they would soon have no choice in the matter. The situation had come to such a point in Russian society that if the nobles did not act soon, they would have their whole world turned upside down when an all-out, homegrown revolution erupted among the serf class.

As Alexander put it, it was "better to begin abolishing serfdom from above than to wait for it to begin to abolish itself from below." He knew that in order to stay on top of this impending tumult, the Russian elites were better off being the agents of change themselves so that they could at least attempt to steer the coming changes to society in the most productive manner.

As such, Alexander II and the nobles spent the next few years hammering out exactly how the emancipation of the serfs would be carried out. In the year 1861, the tsar issued his famous Emancipation Manifesto. This emancipation would not take place overnight, though; it would be a gradual process carried out over the next few years. In this deal, the serfs were allowed to get land of their own, but they could not just be given the land—they had to buy it from their former landlords. This was done through the payment of redemption dues.

Along with the prospect of buying land, the serfs were also given the normal rights of any other Russian citizen, such as being able to get married as they pleased without having to ask permission. Initially, the peasant serfs were ecstatic at the idea that the tsar had freed them. But when they realized how long it would take to make enough money to buy the land they toiled on, they soured on the bargain. Soon enough, the unhappy serfs were holding protests and even insurrectionist riots.

In fact, not long after the decree was issued, the tsar had to send in the troops to put down a rebellion. Even worse, however, the more radical elements of Russian society began to target the tsar himself. In 1866, Alexander II suffered through the first of what would be many assassination attempts. It was after the first assassination attempt that Alexander II began to take a more reactionary approach in his attempts to suppress the Russian populace's dissent. The tsar, who had previously been held as the great "liberator," now reversed course.

In his efforts to bring back stability, he even reshuffled his cabinet, replacing the liberal appointees with more conservative ones. Alexander II also saw to it that liberal and more critical-thinking oriented coursework in the schools and universities were taken out in favor of more conservative education materials.

He also, of course, revamped the internal security apparatus of his secret police. Now everyone was a suspect, and everyone had to be watched very closely lest they step out of line. In many ways, that ever-elusive, universal Russian freedom of which so many had spoken proved to be an illusion. It was nothing more than a cruel chimera of the worst kind.

Chapter 7 – The End of Alexander II's Reign and the Rise of Alexander III

"See though, whatsoever be thy name—whether Fate, Life, or Devil! I cast thee down my gauntlet, I challenge thee to battle! Men of faint heart may bow before thy mysterious power, thy face of stone may inspire them with dread, in thy unbroken silence they may discern the birth of calamity and an impending avalanche of woe. But I am daring and strong, and I challenge thee to battle! Let us draw our swords, and join our bucklers, and rain such blows upon each other's crests as shall cause the very Earth to shake again! Ha! Come forth and fight with me!"

-Leonid Andreyev

After suffering through an assassination attempt in 1866, Alexander II began to focus more on consolidating the Russian state. With this in mind, Alexander II began to engage the Americans over the Russian territory of Alaska. The understaffed outpost had become more of a drain on the Russian wallet than any real asset, and fearing that another European rival such as Britain or France might try to unilaterally seize it, Russia decided to instead make a little money off of the territory instead.

Russia sold Alaska to the United States for just a little over seven million dollars. Since Alaska has plentiful natural resources, some have suggested that Russia was practicing bad foreign policy in giving up this rich territory. But in reality, Alexander II was probably astute in his assumption that another European power would try to seize the land if it was left as it was. Russia did not have the troop strength in Alaska to prevent, for example, the British from nearby British Colombia from seizing it. The United States, on the other hand, would be able to keep the British at bay. So, in this sense, getting seven million dollars rather than being forced to defend the territory from the British or the French was probably a wise move.

Alexander II, in the meantime, sought to improve his position with the Europeans by entering into a partnership with Germany and Austria in 1872, which would become known as the League of Three Emperors.

In the aftermath of the Franco-Prussian War of 1870, which ended with a French defeat, Russia began to build up its navy once again in the waters of the Black Sea. This also came about due to the encouragement of German leader Otto von Bismarck.

This maneuvering would help facilitate Russia's latest round of fighting with the Ottoman Empire when the Russo-Turkish War of 1877 erupted. The war was preceded by unrest in the Balkans, particularly in Bosnia and Herzegovina, which was followed by a wave of brutal crackdowns by the Turks. The harsh measures of suppression employed by the Turks led Serbia and Montenegro to get involved, and they ultimately declared war on the Ottoman Empire in 1876. It was a bold (if not reckless) move on the part of these small Balkan nations to take on the Ottoman Empire. The Ottomans may have been an empire in decline and had rightfully earned the reputation of being the "sick man of Europe," but the empire was still mighty enough to come down hard on ill-prepared Serbia and Montenegro.

Serbia, in fact, was almost on its last legs when Russia felt obligated to come to the rescue. This is what heralded Russia's entrance into the conflict in 1877. Russian forces pushed the Ottomans in both the Balkans and the Caucasus, and by the fall of that year, the fortress of Kars (once again) was in Russian hands. The Russians then continued their drive, moving deep into Ottoman territory until they were at the very gates of Constantinople (modern-day Istanbul) in the spring of 1878.

In order to prevent a complete Ottoman collapse, Britain came running to the Ottoman Empire's aid. The British sent in a fleet of ships and demanded that the Russians come to terms with the Ottoman Turks, which led to the signing of the Treaty of San Stefano on March 3rd, 1878. This was a setback for those in Russia and their Slavic brothers in the Balkans who desired to create a new "pan-Slavic empire," with the Orthodox Christian capital of Constantinople at its center.

However, the end results were most certainly a boon for the Balkans since Montenegro's, Serbia's, and Romania's complete independence had been assured. A later revised treaty was established, known as the Treaty of Berlin, that engineered some lasting consequences for the region. It was determined that Bulgaria would be divvied up into three sections; northern Bulgaria would be independent, but two sections of Bulgaria would be under the administration of the Turks.

Perhaps the most striking term of all in this treaty was the fact that Austria, which was not even directly involved in the war, was given the territory of Bosnia and Herzegovina as a protectorate. Austria would later modify this protectorate status and take direct control of Bosnia and Herzegovina. These developments would later prove pivotal when Bosnian nationalists, who were unhappy with the Austrian administration, began to launch terrorist-styled attacks against the

Austrians, one of which resulted in the assassination of Austrian Archduke Franz Ferdinand, an incident that would be the catalyst for launching World War One.

The Russians were immensely unhappy with these developments and felt that in light of the heavy fighting they had engaged in, they should have had more input in postwar arrangements.

In the meantime, radical Russian dissidents were becoming more and more emboldened, and they were determined to change the status quo. One of the great ironies of Alexander II's regime was that the more he allowed reform and concessions, the more that was demanded of him in return. He may have been the liberator who freed the serfs, but once this was achieved, large segments of the Russian public were ready to demand more—more than Alexander II was willing to give. And the radical intellectuals in the colleges and underground political movements took it upon themselves to force the tsar's hand. Many of these groups came to believe that it would take the assassination of the tsar to spark a revolution. The tsar, therefore, became a marked man in their eyes, and over the next decade, he would be targeted with repeated assassination attempts.

The radicals would finally be successful on March 1st, 1881, when a Russian anarchist tossed a bomb right underneath the tsar's horse-drawn carriage as his entourage passed over the Catherine Canal. This initial explosion did not harm or injure the tsar, but being as considerate as he was, he immediately stepped out of the carriage to check on those who accompanied him. And while Tsar Alexander II was trying to attend to others, the assassin threw a second bomb, which managed to score a direct hit against the tsar himself.

Although he was rushed off to the Winter Palace, Tsar Alexander II would perish from his grievous wounds a short time thereafter. The deceased monarch was then immediately succeeded by his son, Alexander III. Horrified, saddened, and infuriated by what had happened to his father, Alexander III was determined to crack down on the revolutionary activity in Russia.

Ironically, his father was on the verge of drafting a new constitution that would have met many of the agitators' supposed demands, but in the aftermath of his father's murder, Alexander III scrapped the proposed amendments and reversed course entirely. Understandably enough, Alexander III was not at all ready to appease the terrorists who had just murdered his dad, and so Russia went in the opposite direction of reform. Rather than granting more rights to the average Russian, Alexander III became more autocratic and austere, seeking to stamp out the revolutionary spirit by slamming down the imperial fist.

The secret police were unleashed, and the ringleaders of the assassination were arrested. Five of the masterminds were executed, and many more were sent to Siberia. But unlike other tsars, who would rein in the secret police after a crisis had seemingly subsided, Alexander III refused to cease his vigilance and empowered the secret police to take a much more proactive role in daily Russian life.

There are plenty of ironies to go around in all this. But it is worth noting that it was the abuses of the secret police that helped to push the Russian revolutionaries into overthrowing the government. The later communist governments, which were spawned by these same revolutionaries, in turn utilized the secret police in an even more brutal, totalitarian fashion to keep the communist regime afloat. So, yes, there are indeed plenty of ironies to go around.

At any rate, despite the crackdowns, life went on in Russia, and despite the grim picture all of this seems to present, not all of it was bad. In the early part of Alexander III's reign, many technological and cultural innovations were achieved. New rail lines connected far-away regions together, and Peter Tchaikovsky composed great works of music for the masses. Tchaikovsky, in fact, wrote a piece called "Coronation March" to celebrate the official crowning of Alexander III in 1883.

However, Alexander III's hardline approach would create even more enemies for him than his father had. Another aspect of Alexander III's reign that wouldn't win him a whole lot of friends was his so-called "Russification" approach to internal affairs. At this point, the Russian Empire had cobbled together a wide variety of people groups that spanned an immense dominion all across Eurasia. These people groups came from different backgrounds, spoke different languages, and had different customs.

Alexander III, who was known to be a lover of the Russian cultural status quo, thought it was imperative to make these people more "Russian." So, he attempted to institute policies to encourage the Russian Empire's minorities to speak the Russian language, practice the Russian religion, and observe Russian customs. There was pushback against this Russification, and soon, many of the minority groups who felt the brunt of this perceived oppression began to join the ranks of the revolutionaries.

One future Russian revolutionary, Joseph Stalin, who lived on the outskirts of the empire in the Russian backwater territory of Georgia, would be among those disaffected by this Russification campaign. As a young man, Stalin was even involved with protest groups that wished for Georgia to break away from Russia entirely. Stalin, of course, would later embrace an all-encompassing Soviet Union, but in his early days, a desperate, unemployed Stalin, just like the rest of his fellow Georgian countrymen, were eager to get out from under what they viewed as the oppressive yoke of tyranny from Imperial Russia.

But perhaps the most momentous result of Alexander III's crackdown occurred in 1887. That year, his secret police allegedly uncovered a plan to have him killed. The ringleaders of the plot were immediately arrested, tried, and executed. One of the young men to die in this round-up was a man by the name of Alexander Ulyanov, the older brother of the future founder of the Soviet Union, Vladimir Lenin. It was supposedly the death of his brother that sent young Vladimir Lenin down the path of revolution.

Despite all of the inner turmoil of the Russian state, Alexander III did accomplish some things of import during his reign. In 1891, for example, he initiated work on what would become the trans-Siberian railroad. This was a massive infrastructure project that connected one end of Russia to the other.

But perhaps the greatest achievement of Alexander III's reign was that he kept Russia out of war. For the first time in a long time, this tsar reigned over a Russia that was not entangled in foreign conflicts. It is true that at one point, Russia did come close to blows with Britain over Afghanistan, but the situation was quickly resolved diplomatically without any hard feelings on either side. The economy also was doing fairly well, despite a famine that erupted in 1891, which managed to devastate millions in the Russian countryside.

But overall, Alexander III figured that the best way to combat social unrest was to have a firm hand at home, peace abroad, and a strong economy. And as a testament to Alexander III's efforts to achieve the latter, between 1891 and 1901, Russian industry was roaring at full speed, producing massive amounts of oil, coal, and steel. In fact, it is estimated that Russian industry grew 8 percent by the end of Alexander III's reign. It was actually when his successor, Tsar Nicholas II, lost the two stabilizing pillars of both peace abroad and a strong economy at home that the social agitators would create a popular uprising and overthrow the monarchy entirely.

Chapter 8 – The Death of Alexander III and the Early Reign of Nicholas II

"The current generation now sees everything clearly. It marvels at the errors, it laughs at the folly of its ancestors, not seeing that this chronicle is all overscored by divine fire, that every letter of it cries out, that from everywhere the piercing finger is pointed at it, at this current generation; but the current generation laughs and presumptuously, proudly begins a series of new errors, at which their descendants will also laugh afterwards."

-Nikolai Gogol

Alexander III passed in the year 1894 while staying at the Livadia Palace in Crimea. Despite all of the assassination attempts made against him during his reign, his death was ultimately deemed a natural one, and a subsequent autopsy indicated that he perished from a bad case of acute nephritis. Upon his demise, Tsar Alexander III was immediately succeeded by his son, Nicholas II. Nicholas had been born on May 18th, 1868, bathed in the imperial glory of St. Petersburg, Russia.

In Nicholas's early childhood, his grandfather, Alexander II, was the all-powerful tsar of Russia, and his father, Alexander III, was the heir apparent to the throne. Certain in the knowledge of imperial might and the strength of those who had come before him, young Nicholas was perfectly insulated from any uncertainty. But at just twelve years old, he would have a rude awakening, for, in the year 1881, Nicholas's grandfather Alexander II would be assassinated.

After the mortally wounded tsar was rushed off to the Winter Palace, Nicholas was right there at Alexander II's bedside as he lay dying. It is said that Alexander II's son, Alexander III, knowing how much his dad loved his grandson, actually took Nicholas along with him, hoping the boy could encourage the dying monarch to somehow fight his way back to life. As Alexander II stared up at the ceiling unresponsive, Alexander III brought Nicholas before him, remarking, "Papa, your ray of sunshine is here."

Those who stood around the tsar's bed noticed that the effort did indeed elicit a response, as the tsar's previously vacant eyes seemed to take on a look of terrible sorrow at the thought of the precious grandson he was leaving behind. Nevertheless, after having a bomb blow off his leg and bits of metal slice through his torso, inflicting terrible wounds, there was no way that this tsar was going to be able to rally his strength.

It is said that all he managed to do was briefly raise his finger and point toward the ceiling. As his son and grandson quietly watched, the old man's finger pointed up into the air before his hand dropped back down, and he breathed his last. It seemed that the monarch was letting them know that he was departing them for parts unknown.

As mentioned in the previous chapter, Alexander II's death sent Alexander III down the path of being a harsh reactionary. Alexander III took a hard line against all radicals and sent the secret police out in force to make sure that everyone toed the line. Nicholas II very much inherited this legacy, and at the beginning of his reign, he tried his best to maintain the same power structure that his father had created.

But even though he tried to emulate his father, Nicholas was a very different man with a very different character. Nicholas was much more sensitive and sentimental than Alexander III had been. Whereas Alexander III was a natural (albeit somewhat gruff) statesman who relied on a brilliant gut instinct, Nicholas was much less confident and much less sure of himself. Nicholas would agonize over decisions, whereas Alexander III would instinctively act without giving his actions much second thought.

In Nicholas's later reign, his indecision and inconsistency would prove to be his own doom. The boy who grew up preferring to read adventure novels rather than ever engaging in anything close to an adventure on his own would prove very much out of sync with his ministers of state, let alone the Russian people. Ever since he was crowned in 1894, the entirely cerebral, over-thinking Tsar Nicholas II would find it immensely difficult to run his court.

In fact, he often wanted someone else to run it for him. He would find the much-needed support and guidance he so desperately craved from a German princess named Alexandra, whom he married on November 26th, 1894. To the relief of Nicholas, the headstrong woman he married would prove to be quite a formidable tsarina, and in many ways, she would assume a more direct leadership role than him. Nicholas's new wife would relieve him of many of his burdens, but her input would not always have the Russian people's best interests at heart. And even if she did, the Russian people were not always so accepting of her. She was, in large part, viewed as an outsider, both due to her German heritage and the fact that she came into the marriage as a Protestant.

In fact, Alexandra was a Lutheran when she married Nicholas, but she agreed to convert to the Orthodox faith. She initially did this just to respect Russian tradition, but regardless of the reasoning, she truly came to love Orthodoxy and was one of its biggest supporters. Nevertheless, for many narrow-minded Russians, none of it was ever good enough. To them, she would always simply be "that German woman."

Alexandra was poorly perceived by the Russian public almost from the beginning. Even the fact that her marriage to Nicholas II had occurred soon after Alexander III's funeral was a source of criticism, with some likening her to a "funeral bride." Growing weary of the constant scrutiny of the court, Alexandra suggested that she and Nicholas make their family home in a quaint, rural estate about fifteen miles from all of the drama of St. Petersburg.

Of course, being out in the country opened up the royal family to the vulnerabilities of being surrounded and attacked. These dangers were taken into serious consideration, and as such, Nicholas was always surrounded by his own personal army of bodyguards, who incessantly patrolled the property, making sure that no one dared to intrude upon the royal couple.

The fact that they put fifteen miles between them and the palace also meant that Nicholas II began his reign slightly disconnected from the court. Rather than being right in the midst of all of his court ministers, he made them come to him. The couple tried their best to keep up with current events, but this lag of communication would eventually prove detrimental to the affairs of the state. The couple would have their first child, a baby girl named Olga, on November 16th, 1895. The tsar, like almost any other head of state, was looking for a male heir, but he was nevertheless overjoyed by the birth of his firstborn all the same. After the baby's birth, he recorded his exact sentiments in his personal diary, exclaiming, "God, what happiness! I can hardly believe it's really our child!"

Although Nicholas II had been the tsar since 1894, his official coronation ceremony was actually not held until May 14th, 1896. During this much-heralded event, Nicholas had special dignitaries pay him respect from far and wide. There was also a separate celebration held in Moscow on May 18th, which the "commoners" were encouraged to attend.

Here, the peasant classes of Russia were treated to an abundant amount of free food, as well as free gifts. Some of these gifts consisted of souvenir items, such as an enameled metal cup emblazoned with the imperial insignia. It is said that about half a million were eagerly in attendance to receive these prizes. Those that planned this event, however, did not foresee how large the crowds would be and did not take necessary measures for crowd control. The event quickly got out of hand, and there was a stampede in which thousands of people lost their lives.

It has been said that Nicholas's mom, Maria, asked for the festivities to be called off, but Nicholas's wife Alexandra insisted that the show must go on, and Nicholas was not about to argue with her. In the end, despite the loss of life, the celebrations continued, and the only real repercussion for the debacle was the firing of the police chief of Moscow for failing to engage in proper crowd control.

After the ceremonies were over, Nicholas and Alexandra went back to their low-key life, and in the next few years, several more children would be added to the family. Tatiana was born in 1897, followed by Maria in 1899, and then Anastasia in 1901. As much as Nicholas II and Alexandra loved their children, they both began to become increasingly concerned that no male heir had been produced.

Alexandra turned to her faith to help ease her distress. Ever since Alexandra's conversation, she had been drawn to the more mystical side of the Russian Orthodox Church, and she was especially keen on praying to saints.

In this effort, she sought out the aid of a holy man by the name of John of Kronstadt. Kronstadt suggested that she should have her husband canonize a popular Russian Orthodox monk named Seraphim, who had passed away in 1833. According to John of Kronstadt, this monk had performed many miracles, and if the tsar and tsarina were to canonize him, it just might bode well for her ability to bear a future heir. The tsar, who was completely beholden to his wife's will, heeded Alexandra's suggestion and had Seraphim canonized as a saint in 1903.

Coincidence or not, sure enough, Alexandra became pregnant, and in the following year of 1904, she gave birth to a son named Alexei. However, there was a problem; it would soon be learned that Alexei had inherited the dreaded illness known as hemophilia. The illness, which mainly affects males, became known as the "royal disease" because it could be traced back to Britain's long-lived monarch, Queen Victoria. In fact, Queen Victoria was Alexandra's grandmother. Thus, these same genes had been passed on to Alexandra, who then, as an asymptomatic carrier, passed them on to her son Alexei, who was in turn inflicted with the disease itself.

Hemophilia is a blood disorder in which the slightest of cuts and scratches could have one literally bleed to death. Even a bad fall or collision could be lethal since it could result in uncontrollable internal bleeding. As one can imagine, this put Alexei in a very vulnerable position, and if he were ever to become tsar, he would have to be heavily protected lest he die prematurely. Even more fearfully, it was worried that Alexei would not live past childhood to even become a tsar in the first place.

Modern medicine has the means to treat this illness, but in the early 1900s, there was no means of alleviating hemophilia. So, in their desperation to find a cure for their child, Nicholas and Alexandra once again turned to Russian mysticism, which led them to make the acquaintance of another Russian holy man by the name of Grigori Rasputin. Rasputin is an infamous character in Russian history, and a whole book could probably be written on him in his own right.

But as it pertains to Tsar Nicholas and the last gasp of the Russian Empire, we will try to keep the facts brief and to the point. Rasputin was introduced to the royal family by a mutual acquaintance, and Nicholas and Alexandra were stunned by what they perceived to be his healing ability. It is said that on more than one occasion when Alexei was terribly ill, Rasputin could simply come to his side and say a few gentle words. Soon afterward, the boy would have miraculously recovered.

There have been a few critical theories as to why this might have been the case, all of which exclude the possibility of divine healing. Some have suggested that, in at least one instance, Rasputin showed up toward the tail-end of an episode, and once Alexei began to recover naturally, Rasputin made it appear to be by his own efforts that the recovery was made. Others have theorized even more insidious ideas, such as the theory that Rasputin actually did things to make the boy sick and then waited around to take credit for healing him when he felt better.

But these theories do not quite explain other instances in which the child really did seem to miraculously recover, even from the very brink of death, with the help of this enigmatic Russian monk. The main problem that many seem to have with Rasputin is that he apparently lived a completely debauched lifestyle. He was called a holy man, yet by the standards of most of us today, his life was anything but "holy."

Rasputin was a known drunk, and he was also known to have wild sexual affairs with many different women. This is hardly the lifestyle of a Christ-believing, divine healer. But then again, no one said you had to be righteous to heal people; according to the Bible, all God requires of us is faith. If you believe it, it will happen. Perhaps despite his debauched lifestyle, Rasputin had faith in the supernatural that few of us could ever muster or even conceive of.

There is, however, a third theory as to the nature of Rasputin's "miraculous cures." Some have posited the idea that this monk was actually an expert at hypnosis. Many testified to the hypnotic effect of his eyes. Could it be that Rasputin was able to put Alexei in a hypnotic trance in order to prevent him from further injury and speed his recovery?

At any rate, once it was believed that Rasputin could heal Alexei, he was immediately a court favorite, and he would be heavily involved in Russian affairs until his death in 1916.

As his close relationship to the royal family—especially his closeness to Alexandra—progressed, many became quite alarmed. Nicholas II was often asked to get rid of the "mad monk," but he refused to go against his wife's wishes. He most likely would not have wanted to regardless since he, too, was under Rasputin's spell. Nicholas, like his wife, fully believed that Rasputin's efforts were the only thing keeping his son alive.

Shortly after the birth of Alexei, Russia began to face dire foreign policy challenges in the Far East. Russia was expanding steadily eastward, and this expansion brought it into potential conflict with both China and Japan, the ancient powerbrokers of East Asia. And on February 8th, 1904, Japan shocked the world by launching a sneak attack on the Russian naval installation of Port Arthur.

This surprise raid was, in many ways, similar to what the Japanese did to the Americans at Pearl Harbor in 1941. This was a devastating blow to Tsar Nicholas's "Far East Fleet." The disaster led Nicholas II to embark on an even more disastrous course. First, he sent his Baltic fleet from the other side of Russia in a desperate attempt to ferry them out to the battlefield at Port Arthur. The first major mishap occurred in the North Sea after leaving the Baltic when the Russians somehow "mistook" British fishing craft for Japanese naval ships. The Russians fired on the British and sunk one of the fishing boats.

For this reason, along with a previously recognized treaty that the Brits had with Japan, the British refused to cooperate with the Russians and denied them access to the Suez Canal, which would have greatly shortened their trip. It would have allowed them to take a shortcut through Egypt and then move into the Indian Ocean. Without the use of the Suez, the Russians had to go out into the Atlantic and then head south all the way around the tip of Africa, up through the Indian Ocean, and on into the East China Sea. Since the ships had to take this long, arduous trek, they did not arrive until the spring of 1905.

Perhaps worn out from the journey, this Russian naval fleet simply was not prepared for what awaited them. And the Russians were immediately waylaid by Japanese naval craft lurking in the Tsushima Strait near Korea. After the Battle of Tsushima, the Russian fleet was utterly annihilated, and so was Russia's reputation as a military power. However, even with the loss of their fleet, Russia tried to carry on the war by sending their infantry to fight on land.

But once insurrection and discontent at home erupted over the news of what had happened, the tsar decided that it was in the nation's best interest to sue for peace as soon as possible. This led to official peace talks being held in the neutral nation of the United States, specifically at Portsmouth, New Hampshire. The peace terms were presided over by none other than US President Theodore (Teddy) Roosevelt, who helped to hammer out the Treaty of Portsmouth in August of 1905.

This end result of the Russo-Japanese War forced the Russians to renounce any further territorial claims in the Far East. Russia also had to give up the southern half of Sakhalin, a large island just to the east of the Russian mainland and just to the north of Japan.

In the meantime, back home in Russia, the tsar had his hands full with the aftermath of a great civil unrest. The disruption that had occurred between the Japanese assault on Port Arthur in 1904 and the sinking of the Russian Navy at Tsushima in 1905 was the so-called "1905 Revolution." This revolution broke out in January of that year, and it saw 150,000 protesters take to the streets of St. Petersburg and march in protest, with the demonstrators ultimately converging right on the doorstep of Tsar Nicholas's Winter Palace.

At first, the crowd was actually fairly peaceful and controlled; the people simply wished for their complaints to be heard and sought to deliver a petition to the tsar that aired their grievances. Those gathered were said to have largely been of the religious bent and actually sang religious songs and waved religious icons as they respectfully waited to be heard by the tsar.

But even though the crowd was not outwardly violent, the sheer multitude of people caused the palace guards to get jittery. All it took was one wrong move, and someone, somewhere, began shooting into the crowd. Chaos then ensued, and before it was all said and done, hundreds—if not thousands—of demonstrators had been killed right outside the gates of the Winter Palace. This bloody massacre of protesters would trigger a much more aggressive and violent revolution in 1905.

Although some have pointed out that even though the "1905 Revolution" is termed a revolution, it was not so much an organized effort as it was a spontaneous eruption of revolt, protest, and unbridled rage at the Russian government. The situation remained dire for several weeks. After an estimated two million workers held a massive strike, bringing Russian industry to a standstill, Nicholas II was pressured by his advisors to agree to grant special reforms to appease the protesters.

This resulted in Nicholas's October Manifesto. This manifesto had the tsar consent to the formation of a Russian representative body known as the Duma and to limit the power of the monarchy. At last, Russia seemed to be on the verge of transforming into a constitutional monarchy, complete with a house of representatives and a prime minister. But these reforms would only delay the inevitable collapse of the Russian Empire itself.

Chapter 9 – Nicholas II: A Tsar in Crisis

"When the bell tolls three times, it will announce that I have been killed. If I am killed by common men, you and your children will rule Russia for centuries to come. If I am killed by one of your stock, you and your family will be killed by the Russian people! Pray Tsar of Russia. Pray."

-Grigori Rasputin

After issuing the October Manifesto in 1905, Tsar Nicholas II seemed to be on the path toward a constitutional monarchy with limited powers. But by 1906, many of these promised reforms were curtailed in a wide variety of ways. The Duma was oriented strictly toward the upper echelons of Russia, and the tsar could appoint up to half of the membership of the upper house. And furthermore, if the tsar did not like what the Duma consisted of, he could simply have it dissolved and institute a new one.

In fact, by 1907, three Dumas were dissolved one after the other until a Duma deemed to be suitably "loyal" to the tsar was established. The prime minister of this Duma—Pyotr Stolypin—swore to the tsar that he would create a new stable government from the previous chaotic rubble. He famously told Nicholas II, "Give me twenty years of peace, and you will not know Russia."

In other words, he felt that Russia could be transformed into what he envisioned as a prosperous country. And its foundation would be a new, stable landed elite, derived from what Pyotr conceived to be "industrious peasants" who had worked hard, purchased land, and literally bought into the new system.

However, it was not meant to be. Shortly after becoming prime minister, Pyotr Stolypin became the target of frequent assassinations. Stolypin was ultimately murdered in 1911 by a group of unhinged radicals. In the aftermath of his death, Stolypin's assassin—a man named Dmitry Bogrov—would be rounded up, tried, and executed. But even this quick, swift justice was not enough to deter further radicals from rising up against the regime.

One interesting aspect of Stolypin's tenure was that he was entirely against Rasputin. This alone was not particularly unusual since Rasputin was roundly despised by many in the government, but it is worth noting that shortly before he died, Stolypin had launched an investigation into Rasputin's activities. After his investigation concluded, Stolypin sought to have Rasputin evicted from the palace, fearing that he was compromising the integrity of the state.

Nicholas II and Alexandra were, of course, entirely opposed. Stolypin was so frustrated that he considered giving up his post as prime minister. Obviously, there was no need since he was assassinated a short time later. Rasputin himself would meet his end in 1916. Rasputin was tricked into attending a party before being cornered by Tsar Nicholas II's own nephew, Prince Felix Yusupov, and like-minded others who were determined to kill the monk.

Rasputin had allegedly been poisoned at the party, as he was tricked into eating pastries that had been laced with cyanide. He also allegedly guzzled down a large amount of wine that had been similarly infused with cyanide. But when the poison seemed to have no effect, Rasputin was confronted by Prince Yusupov, who allegedly shouted at

Rasputin to "say his prayers" before shooting the monk right in the heart. Prince Yusupov and his conspirators then left Rasputin where he was, assuming he was dead.

In the meantime, one of the men donned Rasputin's coat and tried to make it look like Rasputin left the party of his own volution. Yusupov returned a short time later and went back to the room where he had shot Rasputin. He expected to find a corpse, but he was instead ambushed by a still very much alive Grigori Rasputin.

Yusupov was supposedly completely taken aback by the monk's super-human strength, and with great effort, he finally freed himself from Rasputin's grip and ran out of the room. Rasputin then managed to take off and headed out of the palace and on into the courtyard. It was here that another member of Prince Yusupov's entourage—Vladimir Purishkevich—pulled out his own weapon and shot Rasputin in the head, causing the monk to fall down into a pile of freshly fallen snow. Even then, the hardy monk seemed hard to kill, so the conspirators allegedly tossed him into the Neva River, where he was finally drowned.

Everything about Grigori Rasputin is steeped in mystery and legend, but according to some accounts, he seemed to have predicted his own death ahead of time. He had supposedly warned the tsar that if he was killed by one of the tsar's own relatives—like, for example, his nephew, Prince Yusupov—the tsar and his whole family would all perish with him. And quite ominously enough, the tsar and his family would indeed perish just a couple of years later.

But as much discord as there was on the domestic front in Russia, in the immediate years after the end of the Russo-Japanese War, there were no foreign conflicts. And it seemed that the Russian Empire just might be able to limp on for some time without having to engage in any major altercations. All of that was about to change, though, as the great powers of Europe began to align against each other.

The first signs of potential trouble came when the Germans began to establish close ties with the Ottoman Empire. The Germans had already forged the famous Orient Express, a section of rail line that first reached from Berlin to Constantinople (modern-day Istanbul) before being expanded to reach Baghdad. The governments of Britain, France, and Russia were all concerned over these developments, as they feared that Germany would soon be encroaching upon their own territories.

Their worst fears came to fruition in the lead-up to World War One, as Germany and the Ottoman Empire entered into a treaty together on August 2nd, 1914. This treaty was forged in the aftermath of the assassination of Archduke Franz Ferdinand, whose death led to hostilities between Austria and Serbia. These hostilities would then be picked up by both Germany and the Ottoman Empire. Russia, in the meantime, came rushing in to support Serbia, and France and Britain followed suit. As the great powers drew lines in the sand, the stage was set for World War One.

Despite the dire consequences, many Russians initially viewed the war in patriotic terms and were galvanized to fight. The tsar himself certainly felt that perhaps he could ride this tide of patriotism and use the war as a means of unifying his faltering empire. But Tsar Nicholas had felt the same way about the Russo-Japanese War of 1905, and obviously, that did not turn out very well for him or the empire. It could be argued that Nicholas was a leader who was slow to learn his lessons. And so, when push came to shove, he would take his chances, roll the dice, and hope to somehow come out on top.

Russia did indeed score an early victory against the Ottoman Turks in 1914, when Turkish troops were easily swept back from the Caucasus, with a huge number of Ottoman soldiers killed in the process. But as well as the Russian army performed on Russia's southern flank, it would not fare as well on Russia's western frontier against the well-equipped German forces. And soon, over a million

Russian troops would be dead in what seemed to be an intractable quagmire of industrialized warfare.

Incredibly enough, at its most violent point, it is said that Russian losses averaged at about 150,000 per month. It is hard to even name many of these poor souls as soldiers since Russian conscripts were often sent to the front lines as cannon fodder; they were missing vital equipment, many went barefoot, and some lacked proper firearms and ammunition.

And while Russian peasants were being slaughtered in the depths of the trenches, back home in Russia, inflation was going right through the roof. The buying power of the average Russian had been destroyed, and as it became exceedingly difficult to buy a loaf of bread, revolution was once again on everyone's lips. No one wanted to fight any longer in this senseless war when their families were starving at home. They just wanted to have a way to support their loved ones and live a decent enough life. It was these common universal sentiments of distress that were taken full advantage of by the revolutionaries. In fact, when Vladimir Lenin hopped on a train from Germany and made his way back to Russia to take part in the massive uprisings that were occurring, his main slogan to the Russian proletariat was "Peace, bread, and land!"

Nicholas II, in the meantime, had stepped down from the throne on March 2nd, 1917, hoping that the government could somehow go on without him. Nicholas knew that he was incredibly unpopular at this point and that a large chunk of the populace was demanding nothing short of his abdication. It was for this reason that Nicholas decided to preemptively beat them to the punch by stepping down of his own accord. And upon stepping down, he named his sibling, Grand Duke Michael, as the new tsar to lead the provisional government.

However, Michael ultimately declined to take the job, and soon, communists would be in complete control. They stormed the Winter Palace on November 7th, 1917, and disbanded the Russian government entirely. In its stead, Lenin installed the Council of People's Commissars or, as it would be known, the CPC. The CPC would be headed by Vladimir Lenin. Another notable communist, Leon Trotsky, would be made the commissar of foreign affairs, while yet another infamous communist—Joseph Stalin—would preside as the so-called commissar of nationalities.

The communists wasted no time in creating their own version of the secret police, which was called the Cheka. This organization was ruthlessly used to hunt down anyone who disagreed with communist doctrine. Whereas the tsars were often accused of conducting unfair show trials, the Cheka was empowered to kill people on the spot, with no trial of any sort necessary.

Before the fall of the provisional government, Nicholas and his family had been taken to Tsarskoye Selo until a final settlement could be arranged. As the political situation became more unstable, the tsar, his wife, and their children were all moved to a more secure location in the far reaches of Siberia, specifically in the settlement of Tobolsk, in the summer of 1917.

Nicholas II was at Tobolsk in March of 1918 when he received news that Russia had pulled out of World War One by way of the Treaty of Brest-Litovsk, which had been worked out between Russia's new communist administration and the Central Powers of Austria, Germany, and the Ottoman Empire. Although the Central Powers would ultimately lose the war in the long run and be defeated by the coalition of Britain, France, and the United States, in 1918, the removal of Imperial Russia from the battlefield was a great boon for the Central Powers. But, of course, Russia was no longer an empire, and the Treaty of Brest-Litovsk perhaps signified this more than anything else.

According to the terms of this treaty, Russia would lose all of its Baltic territory, Poland, and parts of Ukraine and Belarus to the Germans, and it would give up Kars and the South Caucasus to the Ottomans. Again, these dealings would be nullified when the

Germans and Ottomans later lost the war, but it was a heavy blow at the time.

Nicholas and his family would be moved again, arriving in the city of Yekaterinburg on April 30th, 1918. Here, they were placed out of sight in a local residence and kept under house arrest.

The entire family was ultimately executed on July 17th, 1918, when the communists in Moscow decided they could not risk the tsar being rescued and thereby inspiring a counterinsurgency of royalists. Not only that, they decided that the whole family should be eliminated so that there would be no future contenders for the throne in the future. It was a cold, calculated conclusion on the part of the communists, and they saw to it that this directive was ruthlessly enforced.

That morning, Tsar Nicholas and his family were woken up and led into the basement of the home. Their captors lied to the family, telling them that they were being taken to the basement simply out of concern for their safety because anti-communist forces were approaching, and they did not want the Romanovs to be caught in the crossfire. Once in the basement, however, a communist officer named Yakov Yurovsky bluntly informed the tsar that he had been ordered to kill them all.

Nicholas was said to have been quite surprised to hear this pronouncement. In a state of exasperated shock, he exclaimed, "What? What did you say?" The officer then coldly repeated his orders to have them killed, and Nicholas shouted, "You know not what you do!"

Then, the killing began. The guards pulled out their weapons and opened fire on the whole family. It is said that Nicholas, who was most likely trying to shield his wife and kids, was killed first, followed by little Alexei and then Tsarina Alexandra. The four daughters— Olga, Tatiana, Maria, and Anastasia—proved much harder to kill.

The soldiers were shocked to see their bullets seemingly bounce right off of them. The superstitious men initially thought that the girls were somehow divinely protected. In reality, the girls had diamonds, gems, and jewels stuffed into their clothes, which partially shielded them from the bullets. Their attackers, almost in a frenzy, began to stab them with their bayonets, seeking to penetrate the jewels that had shielded them thus far. It was a combination of bayonet stabs and gunshots to the head that ended the lives of the tsar's daughters.

There would be later rather sensationalist claims that one of the daughters—Anastasia—had somehow survived and fled to Germany. Documentaries, books, and feature-length films have been made around this stunning possibility. The main claimant was a German woman by the name of Anna Anderson, who surfaced in the 1920s. Many wished to believe the young woman's claims, but in the end, they were proven entirely false. Anna was found to have suffered from mental health issues, and DNA testing conducted after her death ultimately proved that she was not Anastasia Romanov as she had claimed.

Despite the hopes that many had, that perhaps a member of Nicholas II's family had somehow survived, this was not the case. The entire royal family had been eliminated. And with them, so, too, went the Russian Empire.

After the last Russian tsar was assassinated, Russia entered into a civil war that would last all the way until 1922. The two main factions were the Red Army of the communists and the White Army of the anti-Marxists, the latter of which embraced a wide variety of ideologically opposed stances such as monarchism, capitalism, and democracy. Others—especially former army officers—were outraged at the Treaty of Brest-Litovsk, which had sliced off about 20 percent of the Russian Empire's territory.

The White Army was indeed composed of several factions, and they were primarily united on their stance against Marxist communism. The White Army was also the last gasp of what had been the traditional Russian Empire, which was signified by the fact that the White Army actually used the Imperial Russian flag as its standard in battle. Outside observers were reminded of the white flag of the French monarchy, and as a result, they lumped all of the resistance as monarchists and began referring to them as the "White Army."

The Red Army, on the other hand, was a rather motley crew. Most of these soldiers were not well trained, and they were more used to bullying defenseless Russian citizens rather than fighting foreign armies such as the Germans. As such, it would take some time to get them into fighting shape to take on the more professional White Army.

In the early days of the civil war, desertion among the Reds was a problem, and eventually, the communist enforcers resorted to committing reprisals against the families of Red Army troops who deserted. This forced Red Army soldiers to fight, knowing that their family back home could be massacred if they did not. Even if this was an incentive to keep fighting, one has to wonder what kind of enthusiasm these fighters were able to maintain, knowing that their relatives were virtual hostages to the regime for which they were fighting.

Although the Russian Civil War was mainly between the Red and White factions, it was not long before foreign powers began to intervene. In April of 1918, for example, the Allied forces of World War One, who were still battling the Germans, sent troops to the Russian ports of Murmansk, Archangel, and Vladivostok in order to seize vast weapon stores that they wished to prevent falling into the wrong hands—in other words, into communist hands.

Foreign powers actively supported the White Army, and some foreign nationals actually joined the ranks of the White Army as volunteer fighters. Even so, the White Army totaled only about 250,000 at its height, whereas the Red Army had around 4 million troops at its disposal. Again, while the advantage of the communists was in numbers, the advantage of the White Army was the fact that it contained, at least in the early phases of the conflict, more experienced, professional soldiers.

At any rate, the war raged on until 1922, which was when the Red Army finally gained the upper hand. Not only that, but they also managed to retake both Ukraine and the Caucasus, which managed to please some of those still disaffected with the loss of so much of the previous empire. But all of this infighting and struggling came at a high price since twelve million Russians died in the process.

Only after the brutal Russian Civil War came to a close, the former Russian Empire officially became known as the Union of Soviet Socialist Republics (USSR) or the Soviet Union for short. For countless Russians of all backgrounds, ideologies, and mentalities, it was the sudden end of an era and the beginning of a new and entirely uncertain future.

Conclusion: The Legacy of Russia's Imperial Might

Russia rose from relative obscurity to become one of the greatest empires the world has ever known. The landmass of this empire spanned both Europe and Asia from the west to the east and from the Arctic all the way to the Middle East from the north to the south. The Russian Empire had always been an amalgamation of far-flung regions and cultures, and the greatest challenge for Russian rulers was holding all of these different pieces of the Russian puzzle together.

Some Russian leaders attempted an aggressive "Russification" approach to make the denizens of the vast empire "more Russian" by forcing the Russian language, religion, and customs upon those who grew up with vastly different traditions. After the fall of the Russian Empire, the communists tried a more all-embracing approach, attempting to accept regional differences as long as the main tenants of communist ideology were embraced.

Communist founder Vladimir Lenin's mantra was rather simple. He told the Russian people that their adherence to Marxism was about three basic things: "Peace, bread, and land!" For peasants who had suffered from forced conscription to fight Tsarist Russia's wars and who toiled away on land that they did not own and barely had enough food to feed their families, this simple mantra was all they needed to hear in order to side with the communists.

It was for this reason that many Russians turned a blind eye to communist atrocities committed by their totalitarian government. They knew that the regime they were under was harsh, but even under these harsh conditions, there was a general state of equality—at least among the laity—that could not be found in the days of the Russian Empire.

Many have pointed out that the structure of the empire was basically a system that had a small minority of landed elites and nobles standing upon the toiling backs of the majority, the peasant serfs. This drastic inequality of the class structure worked well for future communist radicals.

At its heart, the Russian Empire was founded by absolutist rulers who were raised to believe that their might made everything right. From Ivan the Terrible to Peter the Great, the Russian monarch believed that it was their divine right to exert their authority over all who resided within their dominion. It was only when strange new ideas of the European Enlightenment reached Russian ears that this old order began to be questioned. Then, slowly but surely, an inexorable tide of discontent began to swell in the Russian breast.

Monarchs such as Alexander II and Nicholas II tried their best to stem the tide, but all of their efforts proved utterly useless in the end. The Russian Empire collapsed on its own unequal foundation and paved the way for a communist dystopia that few could have hardly imagined at the time.

Here's another book by Captivating History that you might like

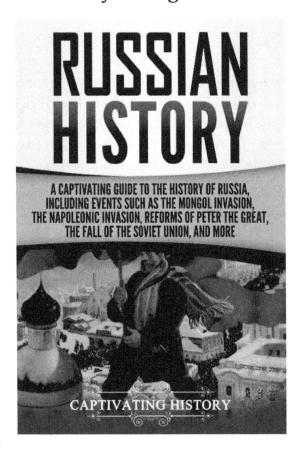

Free Bonus from Captivating History (Available for a Limited time)

Hi History Lovers!

Now you have a chance to join our exclusive history list so you can get your first history ebook for free as well as discounts and a potential to get more history books for free! Simply visit the link below to join.

Captivatinghistory.com/ebook

Also, make sure to follow us on Facebook, Twitter and Youtube by searching for Captivating History.

Appendix A: Further Reading and Reference

History of Imperial Russia: A Layman's Perspective. Anatoly Bezkorovainy. 2014.

A Short History of Russia: How the World's Largest Country Invented Itself, from the Pagans to Putin. Mark Galeotti. 2020.

A History of Russia, Central Asia and Mongolia: Volume II, Inner Eurasia from the Mongol Empire to Today, 1260-2000. David Christian. 2018.

The End of the Russian Empire. Michael T. Florinsky. 2017.

Peter the Great. Jacob Abbott. 2011.

Catherine: The Portrait of an Empress. Gina Kaus. 2018.

Made in United States
Orlando, FL
26 March 2022

16186570R00055